SHORT STORIES INTO FILM

Guide and Reviews

Dr. William Russo
From the blogs of Ossurworld

SHORT STORIES INTO FILM

Dedicated to

James Kirkwood & Jan Merlin
WRITERS, ACTORS, FRIENDS

Copyright 2020 William Russo
book may be reproduced or transmitted in any form or by any means, electronic or mechanical, including photocopying, recording, or by information storage and retrieval systems without the permission in writing from the copyright owner.

LONG TIME AGO BOOKS

Imprint: Independently published
ISBN: 9798689630250
Based on his long-time and popular college course at Curry College, Dr. William Russo presents some of his favorite reviews for the selected films used over many years. Not every writer is represented by each story, but the flavor of the content will enhance viewer appreciation and give new suggestions.

A

ANDERSON, SHERWOOD.

1876-1941

"I'm a Fool."

SHORT STORIES INTO FILM

James Dean & Natalie Wood

A year before they did *Rebel Without a Cause,* Natalie Wood and James Dean starred in a short *General Electric Playhouse* drama. They are callow and interesting to see them before the big time hit big. It was a live TV experience for a Sunday night audience that tuned in for short story anthologies. That desolate wasteland of TV was actually rich and a gold mine of ideas.

So, James Dean plays a teenager with a tendency to exaggerate his self-worth. The story by Sherwood Anderson plays on the idea that youth is often a fool

"I'm a Fool," is narrated by Eddie Albert, pre-Green Acres, and it is difficult to imagine James Dean would grow into this man. Apart from that, it is a cautionary tale with a stabbing pain.

The corrosive effect of lies and falsehoods inevitably do in the young man. And, the stage-work sets add to an obvious sense of fakery all around the actor and character. He is a country boy working as a "swipe," a scatological job dealing with horses.

Meeting a girl, Natalie Wood, led him to try to improve his job and put up a "good front and the world is yours." The fool is no gentleman and has no idea how to be one. He lies to impress, telling of a grand house, rich family, and on and on. He even gave the girl a fake name, "Walter," and can never back off.

He knows he must speak the truth before she leaves town, but her goodness stumps him. He is indeed a fool, realizing too late how one moment can ruin a life.

It's worth seeing Dean and Wood in a love scene and she pledges love to the fake Walter. She will write him at the fake address. Off she went. His lies can never be taken back even 20 years later.

The story is slight, and the production is low-budget. But it is something special in terms of history.

ARMSTRONG, ANTHONY.

1897-1976.

"The Case of Mr. Pelham."

SHORT STORIES INTO FILM

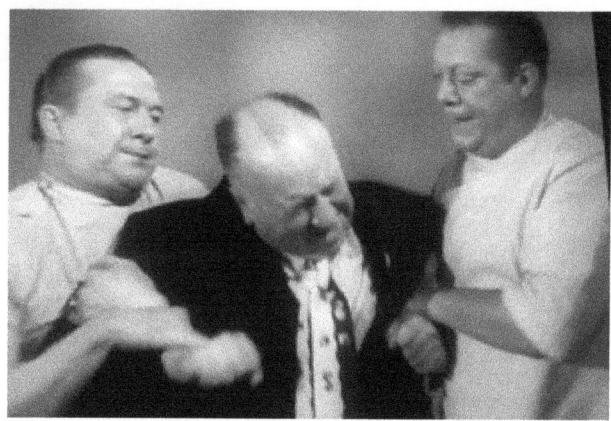

Impostor Taken Away!

We thought we had seen all of Hitch's TV directorial efforts, but we were wrong. Hitchcock introduces this episode of *Alfred Hitchcock Presents* from the first season, but discovers someone has put bubblegum in his suitcoat pocket.

In December of 1955, the series aired an episode called "The Case of Mr. Pelham," with Tom Ewell in a surprisingly dramatic turn. He is an intense lawyer with pedestrian habits and style. This was written by Anthony Armstrong and proved so popular after it aired that he wrote a novelized version of the short story.

As a well-to-do attorney, likely making millions, living a sedate life in Manhattan luxury, with Petersen his manservant, Pelham finds himself cracking up. Something strange is happening in his life. In a prediction of a futuristic issue, Pelham is faced with identity theft.

He starts to discover there is a double taking over his life, using his bank accounts, appearing here and there, doing his job better than he, and showing up at the university club.

Pelham consults another member who is a psychiatrist. In flashback form he narrates the various occasions that he come to realize that identity theft is taking a physical form. He even wonders if there is another supernatural agency at work.

Advised to break his routine, he buys a one-of-a-kind tasteless necktie. Upon returning home, he encounters his fastidious double. The servant states that Mr. Pelham would never wear such a tie—and the man is taken away, clearly insane, trying to impersonate Pelham, despite their resemblances.

As the show ends, Hitch (in a bizarre necktie) is taken away by men in white coats—and a sober Hitchcock says the real Hitch would never be caught dead with bubblegum in his pocket. Off-camera there is a gunshot.

Good grief.

ARTHUR, ROBERT.
1909-1969

SHORT STORIES INTO FILM

"The Jokester."

When James Kirkwood was a young actor in Hollywood, doing television guest roles, he appeared on *Alfred Hitchcock Presents* in a minor role as "Dave" in an episode called "The Jokester." He never had the chance to meet Hitchcock and tell him the Master of Suspense his secret. Hitch had used a true story for the basis of his recent movie—and that the story had been lived by Jimmy Kirkwood as a kid in Hollywood.

Jimmy always looked callow, years younger than his age. He was delighted to have a role on Hitchcock's hit TV series. And, he was cast as the Jimmy Olson cub reporter among a card game of tough vets of tabloid writing. He was, of course, thirty-two years old and a veteran of World War II himself.

The star of the episode was the benighted villain for nearly twenty years ahead, an actor named Albert Salmi.

Hitchcock did not appear on the set, nor did he direct the episode. But, for a young actor, a role on the nearly legendary series in its third season was pure gravy. It meant visibility on an acting career.

For Jimmy Kirkwood it would mean much, much more.

When we met and became friends with Jim, he had switched gears and become a famous writer. He wrote several novels, a couple of plays, and was now rich off the royalties of the book for his libretto for *A Chorus Line*. It had also won him a Tony Award and a Pulitzer. In 1970 in his novel entitled *P.S. Your Cat is Dead*, he presented his own résumé as that of the lead character. Among the credits was *Alfred Hitchcock Presents*.

In 1958, he had not yet published a word and lived in West Hollywood where his father and mother had toiled as movie stars in the silent days. He wanted something else. So, he began writing: not scripts for movies or TV. He had bigger fish on the line.

Friends called him "Hemingway," because he had adopted the habit of writing while standing up. His desk was a lectern where he scribbled his autobiographical tales.

His first work was later turned into two novels and asides for plays. They were fictionalized tales about the son of unpredictable movie star parents who were drama queens. He had already been involved in a scandalous murder mystery as a child. It was his most obsessive experience. He found Reid Russell, a young gigolo, dead of a gunshot wound to the head in the backyard.

He had found a dead body that his mother was suspected of murdering. The dead young man was his mother's boyfriend and lover. Hitchcock discovered a novelized account of this story and turned it into *The Trouble with Harry* the year before.

Jim happened one night at the movies to catch Alfred Hitchcock's black comedy, *The Trouble with Harry,* about a young boy who found a dead body in his back yard. Among the revelations, everyone learned someone else had motive to murder the boyfriend of the little boy's mother.

Since the body wound up buried and dug up several times, the parallels of *Harry* to Reid Russell were startling. However legal, the dead body Jim had found was exhumed several times and reconsidered from suicide to murder more than a few times as the case confounded police. Was Mother covering for son, or vice versa?

The Hitchcock film detailed, with nasty humor appealing to Jim, how everyone was suspect in the man's death. He knew immediately where the story had come from--and that he could tell it as it really was, if not better. "I know what happened or would have happened," he once stated.

Jim said he then bought a typewriter. It was the beginning of his writing career.

He began to write his novel, play, and movie, called *There Must Be a Pony*. It was Kirkwood's autobiographical experience that was the true story that inspired *The Trouble with Harry*.

Kirkwood's novel was published in 1960 and led to comparisons of him to J.D. Salinger.

The highpoint of his acting career was the time he appeared on the *Alfred Hitchcock Presents* television show. And how he loved to tweak the truth, both in his acting and in his writing.

Though this writer never had a chance to see the Hitchcock show until years after Jim was gone, we knew it held clues that Jim hinted about in several conversations.

When we saw it, we were amused and irked that we did not have the information about the show to bedevil Jim.

The episode of Hitchcock was entitled "The Jokester," and featured a blowhard practical joker that goes too far. He justifies his humor by insisting God is the Big Joker in the Sky who oversees our travails.

Playing a joke on an old worker at the coroner's office puts him into the deep freeze as he is locked into a tray in the morgue.

Jim read this phrase "Big Joker in the Sky" in the script and promptly put the term into the novel he was writing that later became *Good Times/Bad Times*.

The entire story of Kirkwood as the little boy in *The Trouble with Harry* came out in *Riding James Kirkwood's Pony* in 2007 from this writer.

SHORT STORIES INTO FILM

Watching *Hitchcock Presents* had solved a mystery of where Jim had found his inspiration—taking it from Hitchcock. Kirkwood returned the favor--as he believed Hitchcock had taken inspiration from his own true story.

ARNOLD, H.F.
1903-1963.

"Night Wire."

Titanic 1953, Based on Arnold's Uncredited Story

H.F. Arnold's short writing career can be summed up as three short stories in the ghostly genre. He was in Hollywood and working with people who could make these tales into movies. He may have seen this as his greatest opportunity for fame and fortune. It could be that he wrote them with half a mind to seeing them produced for the screen.

Not one of the three was sold to the movies, but the ideas were used by other famous horror directors like John Carpenter in his film *The Fog*. Arnold never received credit on screen, but his reputation still towers in the science fiction literary field with constant reprinting of his story "Night Wire."

When his stories did not sell to movies and make it to the screen, he seems to have given up on the literary aspect to his career.

His 1963 obituary in the *Galesburg Register-Mail* at the end of the year told of how his press agent career basically came to an end with World War II. He enlisted in the U.S. Army, but unlike many Hollywood denizens, he did not work for the USO or *Stars and Stripes*. He went into Patton's tank corps. He went to Knox College and then trained at Fort Knox. As a lieutenant he was in the advance guard and wounded.

He remained in the service, convalescing in England until 1947. When he returned to California, he seemed less involved in press agentry, though he may well have continued to dabble. The idea for a *Titanic* movie had come back to life after a ten-year hiatus.

This time, Charles Brackett had the power and the means to make it happen. It may be that H.F. Arnold's last hurrah with

Hollywood was to become Percy White's go-between with Charlie Brackett.

The 1950s began a new era of fascination, if not obsession, with *Titanic*. It must have been an unavoidable shock. From Walter Lord writing a definitive *A Night to Remember* to big studio soap operatic tales, Hollywood movies like *Titanic* with Barbara Stanwyck and a young Robert Wagner looked to the world like a Hollywood version of Richard's life aboard ship.

The story made into anthologies about every ten years since its publication. It has even been reported that H.P. Lovecraft listed this little tale among his favorites.

Whether Arnold knew about the technical aspects of telegraph wires may be irrelevant as is the speculation that he was a journalist or worked on the graveyard shift of an old tabloid newspaper. He was an expert is learning how to use media and press to gain attention for his subjects.

Whatever literal intention the author meant, he was using strong metaphoric language to hide something and to tell a story he did not want to fashion in literal style.

Arnold details how a mysterious and isolated location is using an S.O.S. of sorts to warn the world of their peril. If the years after *Titanic* sank, one of the heroic tales was that of its keyboard crew who manned the telegraphs, desperately sending out messages, trying to reach ships nearby and seeing lights and wondering why their calls for help were ignored.

For over two hours, two telegraph workers in the ship stayed at their posts, tired already from sending out endless and frivolous social messages over the previous two days.

Perhaps one of the most intriguing of details is Arnold's use of the name *Xebico*. It is surely not a real place, and its location has caused many readers to try to solve its geography. It may be quite spooky sounding, but it is clearly an anagram. Twisting the letters around gives you a word that has echoes of deeper meaning.

HF Arnold

"Xebico" likely equals the word, "Icebox." It is a quaint anachronism of the 1920s before refrigerators took over. It is also known as a place of sub-freezing temperatures and an inhabitable world. Surely, sending a message from the icebox could be code for land of the dead.

If you are being dispatched to a watery grave, then your steel coffin is surely an icebox. And, the fog that engulfs you could be the frigid ocean, swallowing up a ship and its living victims.

You don't need much imagination to figure out that the brother—in-law of man who lost family on *Titanic* is writing about the ill-fated ship that cried out for help through its "night wire."

The unnamed narrator of the tale is observing his colleague at the keypad, and his name is curiously enough John Morgan. Again, a person contemporary to the story might immediately identify Morgan as J. Pierpont Morgan, one of the most ruthless financiers and businessmen of his era. He died in 1913, a year after *Titanic* sank.

But, he was part owner of the White Star Lines and had the most elegant suite on *Titanic* permanently reserved in his name. He bailed out of the maiden voyage at the last minute, some said because he did not like his fellow multi-millionaires. The decision saved his life.

According to many reports, he was haunted by his decision to cheat death. He was rattled by the enormous loss of life, including his foresworn millionaire enemies.

These points woven into a short story could be the ideas of any clever writer of the era, but this man, H.F. Arnold, was related to two *Titanic* victims—and he was a well-placed figure in Hollywood. If anyone had a chance to bring the story to the attention of moviedom, he was the man.

And, his brother-in-law was a tormented soul, haunted by watching spirits that oversaw him burn through his inheritance of what would today be $100 million.

The plot thickened as ten years passed—and instead of metaphor, Hollywood was interested in the historical disaster of *Titanic*.

At least one critic succinctly called the story, "truly cosmic horror and macabre convincingness."

Later, during DNA and ancestry analysis, I uncovered the disturbing detail that the family coachman of the Whites in 1890 was named Joseph Shortsleeve—and he lived in an apartment in this house that now contains my personal *Titanic* memorial library, literary archives, and writing office. This book has come out of a room in which Richard White may have visited many times and was the home of a distant cousin of my mother. Who knew?

It seems that Joseph Shortsleeve was a distant cousin on my mother's side of the family, living in Vermont for a time and may well have been in dalliance with Richard's mother. She was alienated from her husband who was away from home for long periods.

Her personal driver was Shortsleeve, living right across the lawn in my present-day home. The possibility that Richard and I share kinship with Shortsleeve, who once lived in this house where we all stay, is startling. Census records were the shocking confirmation of this.

No answers to these perplexing and mysterious coincidences have emerged, nor did I expect to find out anytime soon. My home has its own blithe spirit, and he is happy to call this place his latest stopover while traveling along the grand concourse of the universe.

Titanic Connections

Father & Son Face Fate on Titanic (1953 version).

The 1953 version of *Titanic* and re-telling of the horrific night that is unforgettable and must be remembered was pure Hollywood spectacle. It had an all-star cast, and it ended with masterful special effects for its age. It had to be a black and white movie to heighten its impact literally with the iceberg and figuratively with the horror.

The central family of the movie plot bears a startling resemblance to the real family that became subject of my biographical history, *Tales of a Titanic Family*.

Rich Americans, the father is a prig played by Clifton Webb, and his stunning wife is Barbara Stanwyck. They have two children, the younger a boy (Harper Carter) at odds with his father. Their mettle would be tested by an iceberg.

So, not having seen the movie in dozens of years, we were not prepared entirely for what other coincidences and frightful similarities might turn up. The theory did not take long to prove itself.

The 1953 movie was released in April, on the 41st anniversary week of the Titanic's sinking. Almost immediately upon introducing the mother figure in the movie, played by Barbara Stanwyck, she was identified as Julia. This stunned me a bit, as Julia was indeed the name of Richard White's grandmother, and the name of his aunt, his father's sister (His father died with him on Titanic).

Then, Clifton Webb showed up as the father: his name, of course, was *Richard* Sturges.

They have two children also on board the ship. The elder here is a daughter, and the younger son is only about 14. However, in a key moment, Stanwyck recites the A.E. Housman poem, "When I was one and twenty," about fate. Richard was 21 when he was aboard the ill-fated ship.

Clifton Webb cannot buy a ticket in first-class because it is all sold out: which wasn't true. White Star Lines tried to give away cabins that remained empty.

Though he was a world traveler, a man among many New York millionaires. Clifton Webb's character has greetings for all his friends, from Guggenheim to Strauss to Astor.

Robert Wagner played a 21-year old college man from Purdue. He is a Richard White stand-in.

Among the delightful actors in this film are Richard Basehart as a defrocked priest, and there is also Thelma Ritter as the hard-talking, unsinkable Molly Brown. Brian Aherne seems to be ship's captain in every movie version. Director Jean Negulesco is adept at weaving together an hour of soapish stories before the heavy business of sinking the liner.

In a key moment Barbara Stanwyck tells her husband that their second child is not his. They plan to divide up the spoils, each child going with one parent. It is a haunting parallel to the real family.

The final minutes of the ice-berg's damage and sinking of the ship is done quickly and without any noticeable panic among the men left without lifeboats. They are all gentlemen, singing as the ship seems to blow up and rapidly spirals into oblivion.

There is no bad behavior, or messy deaths, as occurred in real life. We think the smokestack fell from the ship and onto those who jumped off the ship, like Richard White. The unbilled narrator at the end of the movie is Michael Rennie.

Seeing this version of the story seemed to be fitting, as it became tailored to Richard White's actual life experience. Watching was not easier, and not pleasant, no matter how purified the events. Richard apparently jumped off the ship, like Wagner's character. Richard may not have been his father's son, and Richard haunts this writer.

The ghost of Richard Frazar White brought me face-to-face with Robert Wagner a dozen years ago.

BEAUMONT, CHARLES.

1929-1967.

SHORT STORIES INTO FILM

"The Living Doll."

The Twilight Zone genre always works best when the main character is a villain or unsympathetic. Then, when the comeuppance arrives, we have some satisfaction for the irony of the universe where Rod Serling's lugubrious intonations seem apt.

Charles Beaumont regularly contributed his short stories to the series. One of the best takes the latest craze of the 1950s to its ultimate revenge tale for child abuse. Talking Tina or Chatty Cathy was a popular doll of its time, with a voice box and a series of pre-recorded statements. In the *Zone,* this doll has a mind of her own.

Telly Savalas, still in his early career, is perfectly cast as a cruel step-father who would deny his daughter a doll. He is shocked at the wide-ranging and hostile vocabulary she aims at him. No one believes him when he complains about it.

So, when he takes the doll away and tries to saw it in half, we know he is not going at this correctly.

The doll tells him bluntly she doesn't like him. He tries to smother it and lock it in a trash barrel. Good luck with that.

All this simply infuriates Telly. The doll's personification makes him want to rid the world of this chatty, early version of artificial intelligence and robotic animation.

You could almost call the doll a villain, except it seems to protect the little girl, but may well control her too. When the doll threatens murder, you know the half-hour is almost up for this hoot-worthy episode.

BIERCE, AMBROSE.
1842- c. 1916

"Occurrence at Owl Creek Bridge."

Art movie lovers were scandalized in 1964 when Rod Serling's *Twilight Zone* during its fifth season took the French Cannes film winner, edited it to fit a time slot with commercials, and showed it to the biggest audience it would ever receive.

The criticism was patently ridiculous as the Robert Enrico version of Bierce's haunting story deserved the widest possible dissemination. "Occurrence at Owl Creek Bridge," is brilliant whether it is abridged or not.

From its stark opening in a cold misty morning, you hear senses distorted: owls cry in a shrill lament and bootsteps on a wooden bridge make the soul cringe.

Everything is distorted to speed up and highlight the sounds of life that one man is about to lose when he is hanged for some unknown Civil War offense.

Without dialogue, you have the perfect foreign language film.

The escapee from the hangman's noose has quite an adventure during his flight: he stops to smell a flower and revels in the heavenly dew drops of Transcendental heaven.

Despite his celebration of escape, the omens of death are everywhere for those with a sense of doom: from slithering water moccasins to web-weaving spiders, he must fend his way through the dense underbrush.

When he finally comes upon wrought iron gates (akin to pearly gates), he has made it to the place where his wife awaits. Perhaps. The bridge of life goes both ways. That hoot owl may be the last thing you hear in the world, as it mocks your hope.

Heaven and hell never merged quite so much as in this Bierce tale and stunning visual treat of a movie.

C

CAPOTE, TRUMAN.

1924-1984.

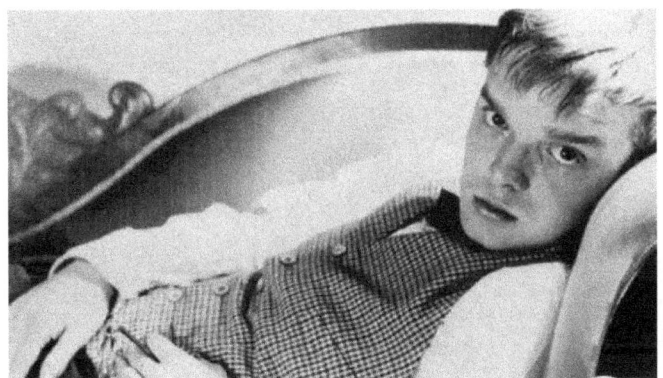

"OTHER VOICES, OTHER ROOMS."

By no coincidence, the production company that gave us Truman Capote's slight novella in film version is called Golden Eye Productions. The re-working of Capote's stories into a movie is called *Other Rooms, Other Voices*, which was also the title of his collection.

Reflections in a Golden Eye is the grotesque and decadent novella by Carson McCullers that helped to create the dreamy Gothic world of Southern decadence.

SHORT STORIES INTO FILM

Miss McCullers blazed the trail that flame throwers like Tennessee Williams immediately followed in the early 1940s.

Later in the process came the world of Truman Capote in that decade. In 1995, long after the film versions of McCullers and Williams shocked audiences with their bizarre antics of sensitive and poetic souls in despair, we find Capote's most peculiar work mis-produced for the screen.

This slight film surely could not have come earlier. It features a fey Randolph, a reclusive Blanche du Bois-styled man, more a drama queen than Stanley Kowalski could have stomached putting moves on Tom Sawyer (not Huck Finn as Capote wished in interviews).

The run-down mansion in the bayou seems more out of Faulkner, but the mistaken tones of an actor imitating the voice of Capote tries hard (and fails) to make this another *A Christmas Memory*.

A marvelous young actor David Speck plays the Capote boy stand-in, and he is hypnotic to watch. Lothaire Bluteau plays Randolph Skully and makes every scene drip with latent pedophilia. It is uncomfortable at best with Anna Thomson as the partner-in-crime female Amy Skully.

Not all child abuse is physical or sexual, as this story unfolds with a kind of slow motion down the drain. And, most of the overt sexual tension of the original story has been watered down with it.

Though we hoped to enjoy David Rocksavage's adaptation of Capote, we found ourselves in need of fresh air and a hot shower after viewing.

Capote's Clutter Story

With a dozen years passing since Bennett Miller's brilliant movie called *Capote*, we chose to look at it again. There were two Truman movies that year: competing for attention.

We felt at the time that *Infamous* with Toby Jones as Capote writing his non-fictive novel was the better. Phillip Seymour Hoffman won the Oscar.

We wished that the two films had mixed casts. It seems each had good points. We remain impressed with Hoffman's work as Capote. A big man, he managed to convey a sense of the elfin Truman. Jones was already the right size, being tiny.

Clifton Collins, Jr., remains so impressive in his work as Perry Smith, the sensitive killer with whom Capote seems to have fallen in love. Casting Daniel Craig in the other movie seems an odd choice. He was all wrong.

As in each movie, there is nothing more cold-blooded than a writer and his greatest work of literature. Don't ever get between them.

Hoffman's fey Capote has a ruthless, cold, hypocritical soul. He lies repeatedly to the killers of the Clutter family to gain their trust. Perhaps the two brutal murderers did not deserve much more than a lying hypocrite to befriend them.

Capote and his friend Harper Lee (also so well done by Catherine Keener) spend hours in Kansas doing research. Without her, Capote might not have a book—and he was less than supportive of her work, *To Kill a Mockingbird*, that she wrote even as she gave Truman her assistance.

We preferred Jeff Daniels as the detective on the case, though Chris Cooper is soberly affecting.

In the end, Capote did not want to discuss much with the killers until they gave him his ending and confessed how they did their murders. He also could not publish his book until they were executed. So, he simply stopped helping them find lawyers—and truly wanted them dead.

The flamboyant joke that Truman ultimately became likely came from his work on that book and his self-disgust. He never finished another book during the 20 years he lived after the execution of Perry Smith.

We still prefer the other Capote movie, *Infamous,* as a total movie experience, we must again give kudos to *Capote* as a film with impact and lasting emotional pain.

SHORT STORIES INTO FILM

CHRISTIE, AGATHA.
1890-1976.

Mystery Maven

SHORT STORIES INTO FILM

You have to delve into the Britbox archives to find the 1990 biography of Agatha Christie done a dozen years after her passing. The thinking at the time was that she was a surprise to have her popularity survive her death.

Indeed, one interviewed critic dared to say he thought she had great staying power and would keep her fame and interest alive well into the 21stcentury. Imagine that!

This is, perhaps, a highly intelligent portrait called An *Unfinished Portrait.* It is based on the title of one of her *nom de plume* works that passed unheralded for years. Her fertile and creative mind is boggling.

This delightful film is narrated by Joan Hickson (who played Miss Marple several times) and features appearances by David Suchet (the definitive Hercule).

Using archival interviews with the grand Dame, you have an understated genteel woman who fairly much is dumb-founded when an interviewer asks her if she likes crime. She retorts, she likes detectives and puzzles.

She worked as a pharmacist during World War One, and learned all about poisons. The documentary uses words from her novels that parallel her personal feelings and biographical events.

IN one creative period from the 1920s to 1950, Dame Agatha wrote about 35 classical titles, all still known. Several include plays like *The Mousetrap* or *Witness for the Prosecution.*

We could list 30 titles here that you'd recognize.

The film is unflinching in examining her strange, staged disappearance in 1926 that cast a murder charge over her philandering husband, Col. Christie. She set him up, or so it appears. She later married an archaeologist, 14 years her junior, who gave her many plot ideas.

Miss Marple was based on her grandmother, and Dame Agatha always maintained good manners in her personal life and in her storylines. She just enjoyed giving people a good mystery to figure out: chess on an entertainment level.
What a refreshing look at the great mystery writer.

Giants in Separate Corners

Recently the question came to us: Why did the two great forces of mystery and suspense never collaborate?

The answer may be surprising. They were both highly successful, popular and beloved: one in film and one in literature. They were both British, lived and died around the same time, and trod the same grounds of creativity.

A few claim Hitchcock was a misogynist: but his greatest collaborators were women (apart from his wife Alma). He enjoyed the works of Daphne DuMaurier *(Rebecca, The Birds)* and Patricia Highsmith *(Strangers on a Train)*.

Apart from that fact, both Hitch and Agatha loved to use the setting of trains for their greatest works! Hitchcock could have directed *Witness for the Prosecution* in 1957, his peak, and most think he *did* direct it: but it went to Billy Wilder who used Hitch's techniques to great effect. Hitchcock could have directed *Ten Little Indians* in 1945, but chose to avoid the Christie works altogether.

Hitchcock told Francois Truffaut that he disliked the genre of the 'who done it.' He found it antithetical to his idea of what made for cinematic story-telling. He likened the genre to a crossword puzzle, with revealing clues as the main point of the story. It was bread and butter for Christie, but Hitchcock hated the notion and revealing the killer at the end of the story.

You may think two of Hitch's intriguing films, at the least, were of the who done it school: *Psycho* actually revealed who the killer was, but not in the way you expected it to be in the final reel. *Stage Fright* was one of Hitch's least favorite films and he filmed it because he was told it was a Christie story, but turned out to be one of his weakest entries.

In *Shadow of a Doubt* in 1943, Hitchcock had two minor characters discuss how to murder each other—and referred to Hercule Poirot, the Belgian detective of Christie, in less than flattering terms.

It's almost tragic that Hitchcock did not direct *Witness for the Prosecution* or *Murder on the Orient Express* to see how he might have handled the material. Both films are brilliant stories and wonderful films, but the echoes of Hitch are omnipresent.

So, we were left without any collaboration between the two greats of 20th century murder mystery. It's not much of a mystery, but it is a tale of audience misfortune.

"Dead Man's Folly."

Two Follies of Poirot

The second of the final season movies for Hercule Poirot (David Suchet) is another of the more cynical murder novels by Agatha Christie. This one is *Dead Man's Folly,* and again Poirot is roped into a solving a murder that his old friend Ariadne Oliver (Zoe Wanamaker) thinks is about to happen at a lovely English garden estate.

The photography is grand and lovely, making even unpleasant areas of the estate (like the murder scene) seem beautifully presented. Alas, as Poirot notes, the wicked killers are about as unpleasant as you can get.

Worse, the victims are more innocent and more cruelly dispatched. No wonder Poirot (and Christie) was starting to lose the taste for solving the murder game. Even his writer friend (a Doppleganger for Christie herself) disparages the writing process for murder mysteries. It's a task to do it.

The film features some of the best British actors in suspicious roles—from Sean Pertwee to Martin Jarvis. Sinead Cusak is among the most striking characters as she plays Mrs. Follat.

This story falls into the latter period of Suchet versions of Poirot in terms of the darker side of human nature. Indeed, even Poirot himself seems to be losing his dapper nature and politesse in the face of increasing deadly apathy.

We can see why the series, after 25 years, is running to its inevitable closure. It mirrors Christie's own mixed feelings about the lark of being a murder mystery writer.

Nevertheless, for devotees of the genre, this cannot be missed and won't be disparaged here. We too realize the clock is running down on the Poirot stories—with their art deco, 1930s classy style.

Poirot's Ignominious End

Agatha Christie's posthumous novel about the end of Poirot fits the long-running series with David Suchet.

Curtain: Poirot's Last Case is a disturbing and cynical finish to the great detective whose use of "little gray cells" so enchanted murder mystery fans.

Over the years, the detective (perhaps like his creator) had grown tired of the evil and murderous ways of sociopaths. So, Christie had Poirot in his ill health tackle the ultimate serial killer in the location where he had solved his first case thirty years earlier.

Captain Hastings (Hugh Fraser) returns for a last hurrah—and turns out to be nearly as dangerous and suspicious as any other suspect.

Confined to a wheelchair and looking exhausted with his heart condition, Poirot seems less the agile crime solver in 1949. He seems doomed, likely a victim as much as the detective he always epitomized.

Indeed, Poirot's anguish over his own role in murder has driven him to religion—as he grips his little rosary beads, fearing killers had driven him to do their bidding.

Nevertheless, the little Belgian has a few tricks up his sleeve as he will stop a serial killer from continuing his cruel murders that misled police to arrest and courts to convict the wrong people.

As a moral man, Poirot may be more distressed over what he must do than his audience. He feels his showboating style has returned and for that he is most guilty.

The final case for Hercule Poirot is brilliant, and he is equal to the task. Older and wiser than when he made his trips down the Nile or on the Orient Express, Poirot came to the end Agatha Christie wanted. She saved her best for the last.

VANESSA's VERSION OF AGATHA

Redgrave with Hoffman

The biopic movie about the mysterious disappearance of Agatha Christie remains a fairly puzzling non-explanation as can be found.

In *Agatha*, the Michael Apted movie is scrumptiously produced and has big stars of the day in the key roles: Timothy Dalton, fresh off James Bond, as Captain Christie, the unloving husband who drives his wife to distraction—and Dustin Hoffman as a no-nonsense American journalist who is hot on the trail of the missing mystery writer.

Vanessa Redgrave's eyes steal the picture as the writer. Willowy, she is hardly like the real Agatha who was a well-fed Miss Marple type. However, there are hints to indicate this is the same methodical writer who produced so many classics of fiction. Dame Agatha seems to apply her writing habits to orchestrating a disappearance that is inexplicable.

Mrs. Christie actually left her child for eleven days—and was dealing with her mother's death at the time of her strange disappearance. Neither of these points is made in the movie.

All in all, the viewer is led to believe this was an insensitive publicity stunt, though the writer may have wanted to punish her husband who is having an affair—and Agatha may be researching how to do in her husband's paramour.

Hoffman is physically dwarfed by the tall, elegant Redgrave, but he gives a sharp performance. However, he too seems to send mixed messages as to his real motives as Wally Stanton, a deceptive investigator. If the real Stanton looked like Hoffman, Christie would have seen her model for Hercule Poirot, a role Hoffman might have played with more relish.

Ultimately, this fictional theory about the incident of Christie's weird disappearance is about as unsatisfying as you could give the audience.

Along the way, the performances are meant to distract and impress. Indeed, they do. If Christie had plotted this script, she would have done a better job.

CONNELL, RICHARD.

1893-1949.

"Most Dangerous Game."

Fay Wray Sees Something!

If you are looking for the prequel to 1933's *King Kong*, you will have found it with this first major adaption of Richard Connell's famous (or infamous) story called *The Most Dangerous Game*.

Right from the opening credits, you will recognize the style and tone of the classic big monkey movie. That's for a number of reasons: foremost, the producers of the Kong and Son thereof films honed their approach to the topic with this classic.

You have the basic premise of a sea captain taking his ship and passengers out into remote and uncharted waters where lurks an island with mystery. It almost seems like the same prologue to each film. Officers are concerned with strange locales not on maps.

Instead of Bruce Bennett (or is that Cabot), you have interchangeable leading man Joel MacRae as the resilient young adventurer. When he is washed up on the shores of a strange island, he meets none other than Kong's leading lady, Fay Wray, who is also stranded there with her brother, played by—you guessed it—the man who gave us the Eighth Wonder of the World—Robert G. Armstrong (not Carl Denham this time, but a ne'er-do-well with the same personality).

They are the guests not of a giant gorilla but of the King of the Island, General Zaroff, (played in slimeball style of the 1930s by Leslie Banks). It seems he has a strange fetish: he likes to hunt big game that is truly dangerous, like people. Back in those pre-Hitler times, he was not a Nazi, crypto-Nazi, or neo-Nazi, but some kind of twisted member of the aristocracy.

With its chase scenes through the jungle, the pounding music, and the production values of Merriam C. Cooper, you have a sense of been-there, done-that, from the next year version of King Kong.

It is a delight to feel the similarity, and you keep wondering where the dinosaurs are.

Not a Cent for Distribution

The new movie entitled *The Hunt*, which is loosely based on the Richard Connell classic story most dangerous game has been shelved or postponed from release. It's been shot dead by Trump and his automatic trigger finger on Twitter.

It now appears that the story about a pre-Nazi survival list is now too hot for Hollywood. They have been a number of versions over the years including some with ice cube being hunted or Joel McRae back in the 1930s.

There was a version in the mid 50s and one in the 40s. The tail has always been a twist on a survival list white nationalist elitist crypto Nazi who has poor people because they are clever and they are the most dangerous game to hunt.

Now President Trump has attacked the film because he doesn't like the idea that billionaires maybe hunting down poor average

Americans, or worse immigrants. He calls this racism of the liberal sword.

This man has no sense of literature, of a Connell story written first in the 1920s as a metaphor of privilege gone mad. There have been versions every generation—like Billy the Kid tales. Each story fits the moment of its production.

If we are learning any lesson, it is that you cannot maligned the reputation of good men who just happened to be billionaires who own 90% of the world.

You're insulting Trump's friends who are holding fundraisers in the Hamptons led by the owner of the Miami Dolphins who happens to have 7 billion or bad craft, solicitor of prostitutes in massage parlors who happens to have $4 billion.

These people would never engage in a sport that hunted down the people who buy tickets Or would they?

D

DAHL, ROALD.
1916-1990.

Barbara Bel Geddes.

"Lamb to the Slaughter"

Reportedly one of Hitchcock's favorite episodes of his show, he directed his old friend Barbara Bel Geddes again. She had the thankless role of the loyal and unrequited love of Scottie in *Vertigo*. For all her dedication to taking care of him, she picks up the dregs at the end (we presume she has little enough self-respect).

In the "Lamb to the Slaughter," she plays a pregnant woman whose callous policeman husband drops by their quaint little bungalow home to give her his notice that he has found another woman.

The presumable victim entitled to be more than mousy over this last straw, we have not seen enough to draw conclusions. But, the victim is Barbara Bel Geddes, and she is nice.

However, for those looking for clues, the first few seconds of the show are telling. The pregnant woman tosses a wrapper carelessly over her shoulder, as if she were a slob at heart in her spotless little home.

We know better. She realizes in a few minutes one more piece of trash on the floor will not be noticed by the visitors she expects after she dispatches her husband with a frozen leg of lamb on the noggin.

After messing up the house like a struggle has occurred, she goes out to the local supermarket to pick up a few healthy vegetables. She puts the leg of lamb in the oven and starts cooking it.

Her sly passive-aggressive plan has colleagues of her husband investigate his odd death, though they know he plays around on a pregnant woman. They are in sympathy—and so the audience even when they see a premeditated murder.

Hitchcock has made the fetus an accomplice in the murder. It is Hitchcock's nasty business at his most humorous.

"Poison."

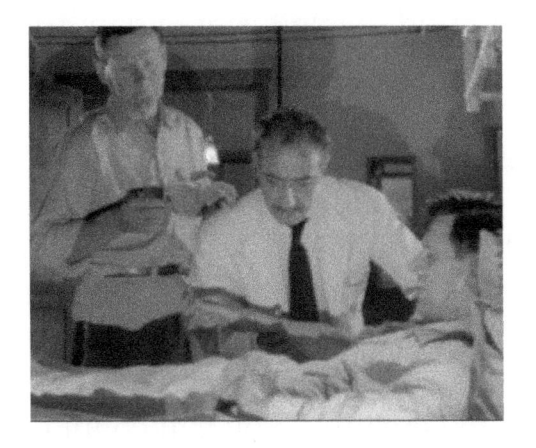

Roald Dahl provided a dastardly episode of the Hitchcock Presents for the Master to direct. Just the season before, Dahl had provided the story for "Lamb to the Slaughter."

"Poison" plays quite well on the denotation of the word. Any wordsmith might tell you there is a great difference between poison and venom. The cleverly titled Dahl story must have appealed to the perverse in Hitchcock.

In case you are confused by the terms, try to remember that poison is ingested and is slower to work in the system through digestion. On the other hand, venom is injected and can have a devastating effect quite quickly.

You may also be curious about a krait. It is a highly deadly snake found usually in the tropical Far East.

Harry Pope needs to pray because when he awakens he suspects the deadly snake is in bed with him. If he disturbs it, and it bites, he will be dead quicker than you can jump up. Unfortunately, his hostile business partner Timber Woods is bemused by the situation and wouldn't mind seeing his quondam friend done in with such dispatch.

Fresh off *Rear Window,* gentlemanly Wendell Corey, usually the epitome of rectitude, turns like the proverbial worm in this story. By the time he calls the doctor and has a few drinks, his friend is paralyzed with anxiety as the audience frets along.

Since what goes around comes around, and a snake is about as likely to go around as any creature, you can count on an ironical ending, as often found in the Hitchcock shows.

Poison may be slow acting, but once in the system, it is fatal. Just ask Harry and Timber as Hitchcock provides delicious suspense.

DAVIES, VALENTINE.
1905-1961

"Miracle on 34th Street."

Macy's Santa & Disbeliever.

Miracle is the tale of a man who arrives at the Macy's Thanksgiving Parade to replace a drunken Santa imposter. He is so good that the Department Store wants to hire him to play the role in the Toy Department.

Edmund Gwenn is so perfect as Santa, or Kris Kringle, that you almost forget that he played homicidal maniacs in Hitchcock films.

He takes an apartment near the store manager (Maureen O'Hara) who is a divorcee with a cynical, disbelieving little daughter (Natalie Wood). Kris Kringle takes this as a challenge to his identity and sets out to win them all over.

The personnel psychologist at the store thinks the man is crazy for wanting to be kind and generous—and issues a dismissal notice that causes an uproar.

Gimbel and Macy, two arch business rivals, even get into the act (with stand-in actors, please). The problem is that poor Kris Kringle is put on trial at a sanity hearing to assess his dangerous qualities.

Notable and downright famous, the trial of Santa Claus is a highlight of the story. The Judge, fearful of public reaction, will not make it an open and shut case—and witnesses must be called to testify. The delightful solution has to do with the United States Postal Service declaring him to be real.

This was always a wonderful staple of the holiday season in American movies, though now it seems dated and black and white, causing a ripple of resentment among youngsters.

Alas, the movie producers and director George Seaton did not foresee the need for Technicolor at the time.

DICKENS, CHARLES.
1812-1870

"A Christmas Carol."

Holly Not in His Heart

Each Christmas season we are inundated with a variety of the myriad movie versions of the Charles Dickens classic, *A Christmas Carol*.

Each season we are invariably asked for our recommended choice for viewing. But, we must defer: our taste in Scrooge performance is sympathetic to the eternal curmudgeon that dwells in every movie critic.

Since we live in a haunted house where ghosts stay with us every day, not merely on holidays, we are less intimidated than most by spirits.

With that in mind, we must offer the best version of Ebenezer Scrooge was by the man who brought General Patton to life: notable contrarian George C. Scott.

His miserly Scrooge seems unrepentant. He is some fearsome in his role that he never defers to the ghosts, but dares them to change him. In that, they barely succeed.

If you like your Scrooge undiluted, George C. Scott gives you a dose for the ages. The unremitting mood of the Dickens London in this movie is dank and unpleasant—and even when Scrooge tends to give quarter, he seems to be mindful of the world he lives in. Scrooge is only slightly moved by pathetic Tiny Tim.

It is the best Scrooge performance ever.

What you see is what you get: there is no fancy makeup on Scrooge, as the only American accent in the cast. Even that is perfect to show a man out of touch with his time and place.

The film remains faithful, almost in every detail, merely cutting away some plot points, though sticking to the original dialogue.

Made in 1984, this Carol is often lost in the Hollywood or Disney extravaganzas. But, we would put our miserly money on this version as the one to scare the holiday spirits out of your classically, mis-remembered moments from the original novella. It's a treat, and not a goose or turkey production.

Ghosts for the Holidays

Dickens with Scrooge!

One presumes Dickens would be appalled that he was given the label as *The Man Who Invented Christmas* because in 1842 under financial pressure, he wrote a little ghost story in six weeks. We always thought Jesus probably deserved a little credit for inventing Christmas.

Having dozens of movie versions of the famous holiday tale about the reclamation of Ebenezer Scrooge, *A Christmas Carol*, it seems only fitting that a charming tale, slightly mythological rather than biographical, would be the latest incarnation of the story.

Dan Stevens, hot off *Downton Abbey*, plays a stylish, boyish Charles Dickens, a man surrounded by his own spendthrift ways and a brood of interruptions in his home, faces a daunting deadline to come up with a novella to make ends meet.

Stories about writers are usually deadly dull and impossible to show creativity, but this film manages to show how the characters, and caricatures, came to life for Dickens.

No small feat is the marvelous performance of the difficult quarry of Scrooge in the person of Christopher Plummer. He argues he wants his point-of-view better expressed, feeling the story is too one-sided!

The cast is up to the weird exaggerations of Dickens, including Jonathan Pryce as the author's father. Many people in Dickens' life take a role in his story.

Cute, by some standards, we see snippets of dialogue picked off the streets as Dickens goes on his daily duties. He hears the best lines and incorporates them into his text. But, it is his debates with Scrooge who visits him in his room that is the heart of the film.

Dickens purists might take issue with the pabulum portrait by Stevens, but this is a sentimental story, intelligently told, without profanity, sexual situations, or other unpleasantness, while maintaining dramatic and psychological effectiveness.

This is a film that insists Dickens did more for Christmas than you may want to believe. Yet, this is more than a holiday fest and more than a simple biographical movie. It is charming, an addition to the Christmas canon.

D

DOYLE, ARTHUR CONAN.

1859-1930.

AUTHOR ARTHUR HATES SHERLOCK

SHORT STORIES INTO FILM

If ever there was a legendary love/hate relationship, it was between Sherlock Holmes and the man who was his spiritual father and creator, Arthur Conan Doyle.

In a French documentary called *Sherlock Holmes Against Conan Doyle*, we have a battle on the order of a duel with the Napoleon of Crime and the Actors Who Took Him On.

Meant to be a money-making enterprise and a throwaway for a couple of stories, Holmes turned into Doyle's Frankenstein Monster.

A marvelous and entertaining documentary gives us a blow-by-blow description of Doyle's losing war with his temperamental genius/consulting detective.

You know who will win this fight. Holmes has survived with hundreds of movies and TV shows, depicted by a variety of actors with waspy disdain—from Rathbone to Jeremy Brett, to the modern versions like Cumberbatch. Thankfully, we never see Robert Downey in the role.

The little hour is chock full of clips of these Sherlocks making annotations on Conan Doyle, a man of some adventure and style himself. Often thought as a Watson type, Doyle was actually more of a Professor Challenger sort.

Killing Holmes was frowned upon even by Doyle's mother, and money is the great resurrection device. After ten years, Doyle was forced to bring him back from the dead.

Based on an old professor who used to wow the med students with his erudition, Holmes was a clever creation who was enhanced by his narrative fellow, long-suffering and frequent punching bag named Dr. John H. Watson.

If you want to see fleeting glimpses of many classic Holmes portrayals, and rare clips of Doyle, you may enjoy the time, though it covers familiar territory.

"Hound of the Baskervilles."
CLASSIC DOWNGRADED!

Pluralized Hounds

The Benedict Cumberbatch *Sherlock* series episode from Season 2 precariously holds on, despite its updating of the original Conan Doyle. Deep down, there remains the essence and core of the tales and characters created by the good writer/doctor.

In re-reviewing the tale of the *Hounds* (now pluralized), all the original features are present, but not in the way you might expect. Holmes is being driven mad by an addiction to cigarettes, and he is willing to do just about anything to have a whiff of second-hand smoke. Even take looney cases.

When a wealthy Dartmoor man comes by to seek help for the mysterious death of his father 20 years earlier by some mythic hound that ripped him apart (and carted away the body) Holmes is customarily rude and agitated. His hyper-manner is hilarious as he displays (showing off, accuses Watson) his brilliant insights into a potential client. We are amused.

The lunacy of the modern update takes hold soon enough.

Baskerville is now a genetic research military compound dealing with bio-chemical weapons. The key may be an acronym as fanciful as any mythic, red-eyed dog-eared monster.

Cumberbatch and Freeman have their patter and interplay down better than Abbott and Costello (surprisingly referred to in the story as space aliens under wraps at the base).

Holmes takes his smarter brother's keycode card to break into the base. Mycroft is now the highest-level military-industrial brain in England. This explains how Holmes can act with impunity and make money as a consulting detective too.

The script becomes increasingly incomprehensible, but flies by at breakneck speed to prevent re-thinking about the logical brilliance of Holmes.

In the Mark Gatiss (he plays Mycroft) version of Doyle, clever becomes chaotic, but it's all in good fun as long as it is not put under the electron microscope. It beats Robert Downey's American Sherlock on all counts.

"Five Pips."
MARRIAGE GO-ROUND

Since 2010 the revamped and updated Holmes with Cumberbatch and Freeman has taken on the true mantle of the Conan Doyle knighted revisions. Put aside those terrible movies

SHORT STORIES INTO FILM

with what's his name, and the worse TV show with the female Watson.

Benedict and Martin are the successors to Basil and Nigel, Jeremy and Edward. This time, to show their mettle, the case of *The Abominable Bride* is set in 1890 or so.

To take the characters back in time levels the playing field with the past great adaptations—and puts this tandem into the canon with accolades.

The Bride case is one of those originally mentioned by Doyle/Watson as too shocking for the contemporary audiences of Victorian England. It is all rather mundane for the 21stcentury, but keeps the newest fans in ecstasy. This case is really *Five Pips*.

Holmes is still disparaging to Watson—and even Mrs. Hudson joins in, knocking those *Strand* stories. She notes she is barely in them. Holmes adds he was barely in the dog story. Watson incredulously asks, "Do you mean *The Hound*?"

Oh, the new old story is juicy, if not ridiculous too. It is played broadly, cleverly, and wittily. Holmes and Watson's modern meeting is re-enacted in gaslight fashion without missing a beat.

Holmes notes how he is a man out of time—and the opening credits are the same as the series, only substituting silent newsreel footage of Old London for the new skyline.

Fans of the British series will be thrilled. Newcomers probably need to watch the earlier episodes to enjoy the parallels and references totally.

Sherlock has made Cumberbatch and Freeman movie stars of the first order—but they seem enamored of these breakthrough roles. We too are smitten.

"The Empty House."

GOOD MEETS BAD

Downey & Cumberbatch: Will the Real Sherlock Please Stand Up?

Sherlock returned from the dead for American audiences this week.

The 21st century version, with all the clever homages to the original, took off on "The Empty House" with "The Empty Hearse," to explain a two-year faked death.

Those with suspicious minds have spent the better part of the canon by figuring out the sexual tensions between Holmes and Watson. Mark Gatiss (who also plays Mycroft) writes this interplay with the aplomb of an Oscar Wilde comedy. Watson has nightmares about Sherlock kissing Moriarty. Not elementary.

Watson has decided to marry a woman during the hiatus—much to the shock of everyone who felt he pined for his lost love.

Holmes may be the most shocked that Watson does not take kindly to being the victim of sado-masochistic sexual hijinks.

How Sherlock faked his death off a tall building in a single bound may be only slightly more ridiculous than surviving a fall off the Reichenbach Falls.

All the delightful supporting cast returns: Mycroft, Lestrade, Mrs. Hudson, Mary Morstan, and Molly, as Holmes must try to work with Watson's alienated affections.

Perhaps the ploy to win back Watson is even more outrageous than the conspiracy to plot his own demise for Holmes.

Benedict Cumberbatch and Martin Freeman (with a Watsonian mustache for some of the night) are more settled and more perfect in their depictions this third season.

If the show has a failing, it is too clever for its own good. But, it makes the re-watching all the more pleasurable. The season is only three movies, but they cram more into them than twenty episodes of that awful *Elementary* series or Robert Downey's flaky movie franchise.

In this series Holmes is an antisocial media star in the 21st century. Norman Jean Baker used to have to dress up to go out and be "Marilyn." Almost as funny is to see the put-upon Holmes put on his deerstalker hat and go out to be "Sherlock" for the enthralled media.

SHAMELESS PBS

Though we basically enjoyed watching the two "episode" commercial for the PBS series *Sherlock*, the documentary by PBS called *How Sherlock Changed the World* is nothing more or less than an advertisement for the PBS series with Benedict Cumberbatch.

SHORT STORIES INTO FILM

The so-called documentary used the theme from the recent series to discuss the Conan Doyle stories. Instead of relying on another PBS favorite, *The Adventures of Sherlock Holmes* with Jeremy Brett that more accurately made the point that Holmes was the first CSI.

The current state of documentaries has deteriorated another level with this hackneyed attempt to sell a series by presenting a film that explores the impact of Doyle's work over 100 years ago.

The repetition of the message over two episodes may be a kind of cognitive device to make sure dumb PBS audiences understand the key point. Talk about misjudging your audience.

To watch some of the most successful criminologists of our time compliment Doyle and Sherlock is indeed heady stuff as they use modern cases to prove how advanced the Doyle stories were. It's true that Holmes may have looked like sci-fi in his day with blood trace issues and chemical tests of evidence.

The best part of the shows included scenes of Doyle being interviewed and explaining his inspiration of a former professor at medical school (Dr. Joseph Bell) who even posed once in a deerstalker cap for a laugh.

We love Sherlock, and we love documentaries that are genuine. We don't love being manipulated shamelessly.

How Sherlock Changed the World is pleasant, but obviously it is a commercial effort to publicize the Cumberbatch series--and that grates.

"Elementary."
MODERN AMERICAN TV HOLMES

Jonny Lee Miller with Aidan Quinn in Elementary

We resisted for as long as possible, but respected opinions convinced us to give *Elementary* a tryout as another incarnation of the Conan Doyle fictional detective.

The American television show runs simultaneous with the British *Sherlock* features Jonny Lee Miller as Holmes in contemporary New York. The two Holmes/Watson series contrast more than they compare. Yet, apples and oranges inevitably remain fruit.

Miller is not Benedict Cumberbatch. The Americanized Holmes is seen in the pilot show with a dominatrix (wasn't that in season two of *Sherlock*?). He has tattoos, is introduced shirtless and wears trendy stubble.

Perhaps the most irksome twist is to make Watson a discredited doctor and a woman. Yes, Joanne Woodward played Watson forty years ago to George C. Scott's New York Holmes (sort of, he was a deluded mental case and she his psychologist in *They May Be Giants*).

The more things change, the more we find that characters in *Elementary* all call Holmes "insane" after meeting him. Yes, he is a high-functioning sociopath, like the PBS version, yet the charming Cumberbatch is not quite the psychopath that Miller plays.

Clever ingredients and startling powers of observation remain hallmarks of the original reborn. Still, we feel like we are watching *House*(the other Holmes spinoff) transplanted in *déjà vu*..

Lucy Liu is Watson in exasperation mode, and Aidan Quinn shows up as Inspector Tommy Gregson, another Scotland Yard cop that the British version has eschewed in favor of Lestrade (Rupert Graves).

The American series is more than watchable—after all Michael Cuesta directed the pilot. It is also more linear than the British version and watered down enough for wide-scale American viewership. Too bad we can't mix and match the best elementals from each series.

Both new versions of Holmes are preferable to the Robert Downey/Jude Law crap that hits the big screen with a thud. It's elementary, Sherlock.

"The Final Problem."

Best Tandem Since Jeremy Brett and Edward Hardwicke?

Not since Alfred Hitchcock decided to make seven-minute long trailers for *Psycho* and *The Birds* has there been a teasing preview like the BBC gives us. Its release on Christmas Eve is a sign that a bright star or two is overhead.

The new Sherlock Holmes (the modern one from England, not the bastardized Americanized one with the female Chinese Watson) will return shortly.

To whet the appetite of the devoted and obsessed, the producers that have not scrimped on clever and brilliantly deduced cases now bring superstars Benedict Cumberbatch and Martin Freeman back as Holmes and Watson. When they started playing the roles three years ago, they were unknowns. Now they have starred in the biggest movies of the year *(Star Trek Into Darkness, The Hobbit)*.

When last we saw Holmes, he was dead in a massive fall off a tall building. Watson was bereft. Thank heavens they aren't consenting adults or Watson would be using the needle out of grief.

Lestrade (Rupert Graves) refuses to hear the outlandish speculation that Holmes has survived death and been in the Orient solving crimes, over in Egypt helping the Cairo authorities, and in Brussels sprouting his line of crime solution.

Yet, he brings a few bric-a-brac to his imbibing doctor friend in his newly refurbished digs. Among the artifacts of Holmes that Lestrade has saved is a DVD addressed to Watson. It cleverly teases the good doctor—and the audience.

We know from Arthur Conan Doyle that Holmes survived his mighty fall, but what magic trick he used this time is still an open question.

Many Happy Returns is a short film that will bring joy to the devotees and leave lesser lights in the dark.

"Shoshcombe Old Place."
Hey, Jude! Sherlock Holmes 1991!

Teenage Jude Law.

When picking a random episode to view (and rev-view many years after first seeing it), we settled on Jeremy Brett's definitive performance in *Case Book of Sherlock Holmes*. The episode is titled *Shoshcombe Old Place*.

Back then there was an attempt to film every short story faithfully. It was something they fell short of accomplishing when Brett died with about six stories left to produce.

The 1991 episode is about a stable of racehorses on an estate. Almost immediately in the opening, we were struck by a young actor, likely about 18, very pretty indeed. He wanted to be a jockey and approached the crusty middle-aged bachelor whose sister owned the estate. The horse master was cool to the young man who looked at him with more than yearning for a job.

SHORT STORIES INTO FILM

Later, one of the caretakers went to Holmes and Watson with a distressing story of something not quite right at Shoshcombe. The sister was very ill, and strange events troubled the caretaker. Holmes chose to dig into it.

With a staccato delivery of lines that is nothing short of breathtaking and hambone, Brett manages to steal every scene he is in as he figures out the mystery.

Jude Law sealed his fame 20 years later as Dr. Watson in a series of bad movies, but here he is most amusingly in drag most of the show—and even shows some homoerotic interest in his boss. Interesting to say the least.

Our ends never know our beginnings. How fortuitous to have picked this marvelous episode for a peek.

"The Six Napoleons."

SHERLOCK RETURNS IN CUMBERBATCH FORM

Sherlock's Smarter Brother: Mark Gatsiss

The new, fourth season of *Sherlock* has reached American television at last with two *bona fide* movie stars as the main characters.

Martin Freeman's Watson seems to be growing into the part more than ever. Benedict Cumberbatch has put his own indelible style on Holmes, but kept him true to form.

"The Six Thatchers" is a marvelous take on "The Six Napoleons," keeping the sharp wit and moving with alacrity in its modern style. From the opening fast-paced, throwaway brilliance of Holmes, the TV movie travels into human tragedy, caused by Sherlock's arrogant disregard for people.

Turning a flippant Holmes into an emotional rollercoaster rider both enhances Conan Doyle's mythic figure and transforms the icon into something not usually seen on the small screen: intelligent, high-functioning sociopathic hero.

SHORT STORIES INTO FILM

All the usual supporting characters are here again—from Mrs. Hudson to brother Mycroft and Inspector Lestrade. They cannot save Holmes from himself.

The modern world intrudes upon us with its technology. Highest levels of government are manipulating the media—and the worst evil of Holmes's world, Moriarty, seems to be pulling the strings beyond life.

This season is extremely short—only three movie-length programs. However, there is nothing old deer-stalker hat here. To wait a few years between dollops of adventures seems well worth the prolonged, pregnant pause.

For those looking for something eventful in the vast wasteland of cable television and Golden Globe self-importance, the series written by Mark Gatsiss (Mycroft as actor) is brilliant and entertaining.

This *Sherlock* puts all the others, big and small screen, to utter shame.

DU MAURIER, DAPHNE.
1907-1989.

"The Birds."

Bird Brains Unite!

Hitchcock's *Birds* did justice to the *oeuvre* of Hitch, not to the stories of Du Maurier who had given him his big first success: Rebecca.

The parts of *The Birds* were far superior to the whole. In fact, as we recall, audiences were puzzled at the end, asking whether that was all there is! The non-ending may be the biggest disappointment.

As for the other scenes in the movie, once the birds start their vendetta, all is enthralling. The film takes about 30 minutes to tease viewers with a bird banging into a door, or swiping down on Tippi Hedren, leaving a stylish trail of blood trickling off her hairline.

Once the crows show up for recess at the Bodega Bay school, you are off to the races.

Different birds for different folks: those flinches down the chimney show that every bird has its own style. We particularly liked the woodpeckers trying to enter the front door.

In another inexplicable scene, Tippi takes a flashlight and climbs the stairs to investigate noise in the upstairs bedroom. It is a wonderful moment of suspense and stupidity from the heroine.

Trying to figure out the motive of the criminal birds is beyond logic. The high-flying gulls set the town on fire and look down with the eyes of a distant god at the carnage they reap. The Bible may have floods, but Hitchcock has seagulls on main street.

The Birds is a seminal horror film for its subtle restraint, leaving excess to imitators who would follow in flocks.

Bye, Bye, Birdies

Imitators!

The Girl, HBO's biographical assassination of Alfred Hitchcock and his relationship to his 'discovery' 'Tippi' Hedren became the subject of a television biopic—short on bio and long on picking at the scab. The film bio essentially recounts filming The Birds, based on a short story by Daphne DuMaurier.

The revision to the story is overwhelming, setting it in California seaside, not England, and giving it all new characters that are instantly recognizable to Hitchcock fans, but not exactly similar to what Du Maurier's fans might expect.

We know who done it right from the start. Only 'Tippi's word survives—and her fury knows no bounds. Her memories are brutal.

Those who love 'Alfie' will be subjected to having mixed feelings. Whoever thought Hitch called himself "Alfie"? We are prone to ask ourselves what's this all about, Alfie?

Instead of the macabre uncle we have come to love, Toby Jones gives an uncanny impersonation of a man who may be more dangerous than you suspect. It's like finding out that your favorite old uncle had bodies buried in the cellar *and* in the closet.

Several times we became breathless at the remarkable depiction by Jones of his Hitch character (following in his Truman Capote footsteps of a few years ago).

The beautiful Miss 'Tippi' Hedren enjoyed a sympathetic interpretation by Sienna Miller, not a slouch at all in the beauty department. However, at least a dozen times we were struck at her resemblance to Janet Leigh in *Psycho,* not the small-features we adored on the face of Miss Hedren.

Hedren was handpicked to play the lead in *The Birds.* She was a New York model, not an actress. But under the tutelage of Hitch, she became a puppet in the mode of Pinocchio and Petroushka. She wanted to be a movie star, whatever the cost—and the price extracted by Hitchcock was more than any star like Grace Kelly or Kim Novak would have tolerated.

The movie tale attributed no storyline to anyone other than writer Gwyneth Hughes, though the heavy hand of Hedren seems to have the last say.

Hitch is gone, unable to defend his reputation, though we would not be surprised at the accuracy of the slimy Limey depiction and attitude.

Hitch often looks like he is about to stalk Hedren and accost her in the shower with a large knife.

Directors may do much to achieve the effects they desire. If so, Hitchcock was ruthless and cruel, sociopathic and cold-blooded, like a Ripper editing celluloid.

It's worth examining an alternative view of the Master. This movie isn't *Vertigo*. It isn't even in the class of *Marnie*, no masterpiece from the Master, despite the statement on the final credits.

F

FITZGERALD, F. SCOTT.
1896-1940

"Bernice Bobs Her Hair."

SHORT STORIES INTO FILM

Perhaps the most condemning criticism of stories like "Bernice Bobs Her Hair" is that they are now read and taught as part of historical literary classes in a few colleges where the professor dares to be bold.

Unlike William Faulkner whose literary depiction include Southern blacks, Fitzgerald dealt more with upper-crust and privileged white people. So, he is still on the dance card, with novels like The Great Gatsby. There's enough privilege he criticized and now readers can join in the free-for-all. So, when you have a quaint 1920s tale of a girl who bucks the system and wants to bob her hair, it takes on the early women's rights movement. She is now a preliminary adolescent Suffragette.

It may be the only way to sell Fitzgerald's literary *oeuvre* nowadays.

The notion of debutantes is nearly as quaint as loose sexuality evident by girls who cut their hair to a male style. This was the Jazz Age and teens fought to be adults, and women fought to be treated as equal rights citizens.

The film with Shelley Duvall manages to be a set designer dream with its objects and props to epitomize the privilege of living in a Wisconsin suburb of some wealth.

The real tragedy of this tale and its little movie equivalent is that it has been reduced to being a high school literary project. Outside that venue, you may have few takers no matter how high quality the TV movie production comes across.

High school English classes may be one of the few places where make-overs and teenage rituals are of any interest to anyone.

If you see dancing rituals as a foil for today's hip-hoppers, you have a jealous girl named Marjorie who is not about to lose her boyfriend or ability to attract one to an odd stick named Bernice.

H

HALE, EDWARD EVERETT.
1822-1909.

Cliff Robertson in title role with Robert Ryan.

"Man without a Country."

My grandfather told me a story about how he used to see old Edward Everett Hale, nephew of patriot Nathan Hale, doddering around Beacon Hill in a stove-pipe hat in his old age. Kids used to throw snowballs at him to try to knock off his hat. I was appalled even as a kid.

Hale's cautionary tale about what it is to be a patriot may now be deader than a doornail with political factions now upending the Constitution of the United States. But, once upon a time, this story had deeper resonant meaning.

Part of the Aaron Burr plot to overthrow the new American government, Philip Nolan is put on trial for sedition and treason. During his trial he states, "Damn the United States. I wish I never heard of the United States." To which the tribunal gives him what he wishes for: he will be put aboard a ship never to set port in the US. No one must ever speak the words "United States of America," to him, nor may he see any documents that contain such words.

He scoffs at the sentence in 1807, but when his obituary is printed during the Civil War, his room is discovered to have a map of the US he has drawn and filled with info people have secretly given him over the years.

During the War of 1812, he takes an officer's role in a battle and saves the ship for the United States, but there will be no commutation. He is damned.

One of the most versatile of actors plays Nolan: Cliff Robertson who was at home in costume, in modern togs, or any other permutation. His aging Nolan is dignified and he suffers in nobility when one woman pointed notes when he asks her of home: "I thought you were the man who never wanted to hear of home."

Costars are top notch, like Robert Ryan, never a disappointment, and Beau Bridges, back in 1973. It remains a film with an abject message.

He learns even from slaves being transported to the United States over the years. He must serve his punishment in true Hemingway fashion. It is more interesting that few film-makers wanted to make this as a movie—and it fell to a TV production with a low budget.

HALL, EDMUND NORTH.
1911-1990.

"Day the Earth Stood Still"

Gort (foreground) with Klaatu.

Coming at the onset of the flying saucer craze after Roswell in 1947, *The Day the Earth Stood Still* was monumental in its influence and popularity.

In all likelihood, that composer Bernard Herrmann used the computerized sound of a theremin for the haunting music score also gave this movie and story something extra.

Edmund North Hall's original story was darker and more modern than the dark and hopeful tale of an alien coming to Earth to save us all from ourselves.

You will always remember the strange metallic robot with the power of life and death as a galaxy policeman. His ray from the visor instantly melts you into oblivion. Gort is not to be trifled with, and it may be the only kind of power that humankind understands.

SHORT STORIES INTO FILM

Michael Rennie made a splash as Klaatu, the spaceman who sounds like he is from Boston (one of the characters comments on Klaatu's New England accent) and looks odd enough to pass as a person from another world. His nemesis is Frank Conroy as the government official; he played the fake Confederate lynch mob leader in *Ox Bow Incident*. He seems typecast. Patricia Neal is the woman who befriends the odd messenger from space.

Klaatu calls himself Mr. Carpenter, which is heavy-handed for Christ imagery, but quite acceptable in sci-fi. Director Robert Wise can handle child actors and robotic special effects with equal adeptness.

Earthling friends of Klaatu tell him he needs a clever idea as symbolism to make people accept his message. And, the idea is highly entertaining: he will stop all mechanical activity for 30 minutes to demonstrate the power of other creatures in the universe.

You need something special to withstand 70 years and a remake of the movie. This black and white gem still gleams with its United Nations warning.

HARTE, BRET.
1836-1902.

"Emperor Norton's Bridge."

SHORT STORIES INTO FILM

Edgar Stehli as Emperor Norton with actor Jan Merlin.

Recently we heard from the "Emperor's Bridge Campaign" in San Francisco and its president, John Lumea. They are a historical group that has amassed a collection of memorabilia about Emperor Norton, a 19th century citizen who was considered pixilated, but clairvoyant about the future.
It seems my old collaborator and dear friend, Jan Merlin, appeared on a TV show in 1956 that detailed Emperor Norton's life. Jan played another writer by the name of Bret Harte.

After his acting career, Jan had a prolific writing career, even winning an Emmy for television writing. We always thought he was Bret Harte's equal.

So, when we received a pristine copy of an old *Telephone Time* TV show, we were eager to view it. We had seen it 30-odd years ago. We know that Jan Merlin never really had a chance to watch his performances on television in those days.

Merlin was too busy each week, preparing for the next role, as he was active in dozens of TV shows and feature films in far-flung places like Kenya with Ann Sheridan. He saw many shows only a few years ago. Some he has never seen. This appearance was a rare sympathetic role. Usually he was a baddie in TV westerns—and plugged at the last minute of the show—and showdown.

Sixty years later, Jan still looks much the same, still youthful, but is now in his retirement, probably the only survivor of that long-ago show on Norton with the exception of a child actress, Cheryl Callaway, who had a scene.

Edgar Stelhi played Emperor Norton. We almost didn't recognize him with his Trump-style wig. He also was quite active on television in the 1950s. His best role in movies was opposite Audie Murphy as the old judge in *No Name on the Bullet.* Jan also did a couple of movies with Audie—and his TV show too as a guest.

A 25-minute teleplay was chock full of intriguing moments, including a scene in which Norton is mocked in a saloon with a fake crown and seated among his detractors; it reminded one of those Renaissance paintings on the mocking of Christ by his captors.

Owing to the vigilance of Jan's character, Norton's past is revealed—and he wins accolades for his ideas.

Now a San Francisco group has taken up Norton's cause, to the point of hoping to rename a section of the Bay Bridge after the old emperor.

Old TV shows never die. They end up in media museums, awaiting re-discovery.

HEMINGWAY, ERNEST.

1899-1961.

"The Killers."

Burt Lancaster Awaits the Grim Reapers.

A late 1940s film noir version of "The Killers" made author Ernest Hemingway wince. He was hypercritical of the Hollywood versions of his novels and stories.

Yet, the star vehicle for Ava Gardner and Burt Lancaster used the first twenty-minutes to tell the short story. The rest is Hollywood explanations that have nothing to do with Hemingway except to build off his message.

The original dark opening seems to tell an inexplicable tale of a gas station attendant who is hunted down by two hired gunmen. Instead of running when he is warned, he simply waits for the inevitable killing.

When asked why he won't flee, he gives the ultimate Hemingway man's answer. There comes a time when you stop running because it doesn't matter in the end.

The moody and eerie tale is brilliantly directed by Robert Siodmak and were it a short subject could have been a masterpiece after the killers climb the boarding house stairs and let their bullets fly.

Young Burt Lancaster is suitably tough and handsome, as you'd want you hero, but he is antiheroic in not fighting. The rest of the movie is a pathetic attempt to flashback to his roots and how he upset the mobsters.

Quiet nighttime moments in an old-fashioned diner and the ominous sense the Swede's friends have about the mystery visitors is all part of the philosophical insight of the author.

Many questions about the Swede are raised and there are no answers. It was always the style of Hemingway to omit key information: you fill in the blanks. Sometimes if you have enough questions, they provide an answer. The central mystery of the Swede is explained in banal terms during the remainder of the movie.

Hemingway gives you suspense in the anticipation of answers, but you will be thwarted and left to your own devices to figure out the moral of the story.

"Old Man and the Sea."

Hemingway hated this film, mainly because of Spencer Tracy, not exactly a Cuban fisherman type. However humble Mr.

Tracy tried to show himself, he was either Father Flanagan, Thomas Edison, playing the Great Agnostic, or as Clark Gable's buddy. He was not an illiterate fisherman whose dignity was tied up in a fish story.

Nowadays, most younger viewers have no idea who this old man is (forget the Katharine Hepburn angle), and objectively, he seems unpretentious—and rather dynamic in flashbacks to his youth. A generation later another actor named Anthony Quinn tried his hand at the role, but he was even more mannered.

Hemingway likes to play off big prefigures—ocean, youth, and won a Nobel Literary Prize for the narrative simplicity. Tracy hardly ever fulfilled the Seven Cardinal Virtues in his personal life, and it may be why he does such a good job showing them in the Old Man.

It was said that Tracy wanted badly to play this character because he felt that his own life was one of great tragedy and trying effort. He suffered in his marriage, his love life, and may have felt tired and defeated by the empty celebrity of acting. He seemed to accept better than most the bad luck that befell the old fisherman. Despite his personal alcoholism, Tracy felt he needed to prevail in defeat, like the Hemingway character.

The Old Man thinks of his quarry, the Marlin, as a symbolic brother that he has no compunction about catching. Alone in a small boat, it is folly in an ocean filled with sharks, the perfect predator and villain.

You may come out thinking that biology is the most powerful force in the story—and to fight it is folly, but the fight is what

Hemingway allegedly cherished, despite his cop-out suicide as the ravages of time crept up on him.

I

IRVING, WASHINGTON.
1783-1859.

"Legend of Sleepy Hollow"

SHORT STORIES INTO FILM

One of the great travesties of movie history is that there have been many versions of the Legend of Sleepy Hollow or The Headless Horseman, and not one of them was any good.

Producers and actors have been selective and choosy about what details go into what versions. You have Ichabod Cranes who are young, middle-aged, athletic, handsome, and nothing like the gangly schoolmaster who lacked humor.

The headless horseman is reduced to Halloween hijinks and a pumpkin head he tosses all too freely.

Ichabod has been played by Will Rogers in 1923 in a silent version, and in some atrocity with Johnny Depp in recent years in which there is NO connection to the original story. Depp's Crane is a forensic pathologist from New York.

It is one of the Knickerbocker Tales, one of the first collection of great American literature that included Rip Van Winkle's story.

Washington Irving wrote his story with a wink and nod to the headless horseman. Most versions play it as real, not paranormal, and not as a gag done by local men to tease the prissy schoolmaster.

We even saw a version with Ichabod played by a dog. It has been done in animation, on the big screen, for TV, as a special, as an episode of children's tales. We have heard crooner Bing Crosby doing a Disney version.

Everyone finds the story in the public domain and can rip it to shreds.

Whatever would Washington Irving make of all this drivel?

J

JAMES, HENRY.
1843-1916.

Perfectly Cybill!

"Daisy Miller."

As mentor to the star, director, creative force, and whiz kid, young Peter Bogdanovich took dry Henry James and made a fast-moving, emotionally-moving film of a famous novella, *Daisy Miller*.

You could not find a more perfect American girl than Cybill Shepherd as Daisy: unspoiled, direct, and completely at odds with social conventions in 19th century Europe.

Caught between women like her scatter-brained mother (Cloris Leachman) and an American social doyen Mrs. Walker (Eileen Brennan), Daisy does not stand a chance if she ignores or simply teases Frederick Winterbourne (brilliant young Barry Brown, too soon gone to a premature grave), an American who is a permanent resident of Europe.

Whether it's going on a tourist trip to Byron's famous castle without chaperone, or worse, going to the place of the viral Roman fever at the Colosseum, Daisy is hell-bent on living her way. Extraordinary location filming makes this a treat.

Winterbourne resists the notion that her scandalous behavior is anything bad. Yet, he cannot convince others in his social set— and crumbles in their heavy pressure.

Rich Americans policed themselves to try to avoid any ugly American image. Fast-talking Daisy, flirtatious and coy, breaks all the rules in her *nouveau riche niche*.

If Daisy learns there is a social convention, she is hell-bent on testing its merits. What she does not expect is that she will be shunned by the Americans living abroad. To a social butterfly, as Cybill Shepherd delineates to a T, this is far more damaging than she expects.

Perhaps this quintessential American girl could bear all if only Winterbourne remained on her side. He is sorely tested, and ultimately as the laconic Barry Brown narrates, he has lived too long in foreign places.

Alas, it is Brown, the actor, who is gone too soon, based on the promise of this extraordinary film performance.

"The Heiress."

SHORT STORIES INTO FILM

Scene Not in Movie!!!

Like Somerset Maugham years later, Henry James was a devout listener to gossip that gave him plenty of insights into human nature. His short story "Washington Square" was transformed into a play called *the Heiress* and later a lesser film version in color.

The earlier version had a stunning cast and an emotional wallop from director William Wyler, yet again. Olivia De Havilland plays a mousy heiress, brow-beaten by her aunt and widower father (another acid portrait by Ralph Richardson).

The story is set in the upper crust world of New York society in the 19th century. She meets a gold-digging fortune hunter who is more beautiful than everyone else: young Montgomery Clift at his most stunning. Her father determines he is only interested in his banal daughter for her inheritance.

Whether Dr. Sloper is right that Catherine is ripe for fortune hunters may be moot when it comes to her pathetic life. He wants to protect her and separate her from such men, perhaps any man not rich enough.

This could be a novella of manners—except for so many cruel twists. Catherine is prepared to run away, penniless, to escape her father's clutches. But Morris, her suitor, simply leaves her in the lurch. She must eat crow and remain humiliated by her father. Yet, there is now within her a desperate hatred of both men.

James likely heard the story of a woman who sat in the park, refusing to go to dying father's bedside. It was the spark for the story. She also finds her tongue at one point—telling off Dr. Sloper in no uncertain terms.

That is merely penultimate: the best revenge is saved for Morris when he returns years later, greedier and more desperate. This movie provides a catharsis for sure, but it is bittersweet. Performers are beyond perfection.

"Aspern Papers."

Meyers out of element.

SCANDALOUS TALE

French director Julien Landais brings his rococo style to the proceedings of the Henry James tale with his usual interest in Dopplegangers (Jonathan Rhys Meyers has the same blue eyes as Alain-Fabien Delon and the director himself). He seems obsessed with his own stunning looks. He is not into playing someone of the story's timeframe.

The sly novella by the master of manners and psychology, Henry James, is well-played out in *The Aspern Papers*. As Morton

Vint, Jonathan Rhys-Meyers is suitably shady as a snooping researcher. He is anachronistic in posture and demeanor (going hatless and with bohemian friends of the 1880s in Venice). He seems to hang around with a bunch of lesbians (shades of *the Bostonians*).

He wants the love letters of an aging woman and will stop at nothing to put his hands on them. There is no kill-fee here, and he is the progenitor of *National Enquirer* dirty deeds even back in the 19th century.

Yes, this is a literary film in the Ivory-Merchant mode. Indeed, James Ivory is executive producer—and all the old style is brought back with a cutting edge of nastiness for the 21st century with a young French director in charge.

When the *poseur* earns that all the papers are hidden by Juliana, one-time lover of Jeffrey Aspern (likely Percy Shelley based on details), he is moved to become ruthless in putting his grubby hands on them.

There is a dark secret here, often hinted broadly in flashbacks that Aspern was bisexual—with a Byronic friend—and Juliana.

All this adds to the charades played by each of the characters.

Joely Richardson (Vanessa Redgrave's daughter) plays her dull, spinster niece here with no pretense of acting out the role of her aunt every night—as the earlier version with Susan Hayward showed. The old lady was likely Mary Shelley's sister, Claire Claremont, who had "everything" when it comes to memorabilia of dead poets.

SHORT STORIES INTO FILM

You may recognize strands of Wagner's *Tristan & Isolde* before it blows into a full-force cliché to end the movie. It is effective, nevertheless. Here too the ring of Jeffrey Aspern, as in the earlier version, plays an intriguing role as the spinster niece puts a deal to the devil publisher if he wants the literary treasure.

Landais gives us a stunner for his full-length first effort, providing us with a controlled *tour-de-force* that makes us anticipate his next film. Brilliant, complex work.

LONDON, JACK.
1876-1916

"To Build a Fire"

"To Build a Fire," Jack London's philosophic Naturalism short story is regarded highly among his writings, often considered a better condensed version of his novels. So, an hour-long movie version, no matter how well made, will have London fans in a tizzy.

This version, directed in 1969 by David Cobham, features the high-powered narrative voice of Orson Welles. Without ever appearing in the movie, Welles is a force through his intonations.

Many believe his objective narrator undercuts the first-person deadpan words of London. In fact, Welles manages not to be condescending, but the main character is out in 50-degree below zero temperatures in the Klondike.

So, when Welles notes that man did not understand the significance of cold, you have to agree. London liked to show adventurous men who were unprepared to meet the challenge of a cruel world, but went forging ahead.

Here, the Gold Rush only adds to the greedy motivations of men with a chip on their shoulder. The man even disparages his dog, ironically called Pepper in the movie, for his common sense at realizing the man is a fool.

The human condition is frailty, and Nature is harsh. It seems rather self-evident. Cold and wet feet are a doomsday event when you're alone in the wilderness. And, the man ignored the voice of experience of an elder who said never to go out alone.

Welles has a tone that becomes less objective and snider in its gentle way about the ultimate failure of man to build a fire to save himself. London always seemed to prefer good instincts to intelligence, and as in many stories of London, he thinks more of the dog than his human counterpart.

Film is never a directly comparable metaphor to literature, but veers off in its own ways under a director who interprets the words of the writer.

If you find this film wanting, you may want to re-read the story. Man was never dog's best friend, and you will be happy for the dog's situation at climax. The dog is more than a foil

M

MATHESON, RICHARD.
1926-2013.

"The Invaders."

LITTLE SPACE ALIENS ON THE MOVE!

SHORT STORIES INTO FILM

Shatner Wings It!

Back in the 1950s and 1960s, intelligentsia thought TV was rotting the mind, but two anthology series were keeping the American short *story alive: Alfred Hitchcock Presents* and *Twilight Zone*.

Richard Matheson wrote for both and made a name for himself in the process. For Rod Serling's series, he adapted over a dozen of his stories for the half-hour surprise ending show.

Two of his most famous include well-known TV stars in lead guest roles: William Shatner did "Nightmare at 20,000 Feet," and Agnes Morehead did "The Invaders."

Both are remarkable and only does Shatner's episode seem a tad dated (guns aboard a commercial airliner soon went less than ballistic). He faced a gremlin no one else saw as they flew at night into the *Twilight Zone*.

Morehead's show is more interesting for its lack of dialogue and ability to turn an unsympathetic figure into one of great suffering as she plays a haggard witch-like figure out in a cabin in the wilderness. She suffers an attack of small spacemen who crash land on her house's roof.

The farmhouse is timeless by its primitive qualities, lacking electricity or modern convenience. It is also a dank place of ominous features. When you are an old woman living alone, you had better be resilient.

Morehead's groaning and sounds of effort make her downright heroic. She is wounded in the process of fighting off these little men from space in bloated tiny spacesuits. She kicks and stabs at them, but they keep attacking.

When she finally climbs up to the roof to confront their crashed flying saucer, it is we who are horrified, not her. Oh, that *Twilight Zone* twist. Wonderful to see Matheson's story done with such a marvelous lack of sci-fi effects. "Invaders" is a superior bit of entertainment.

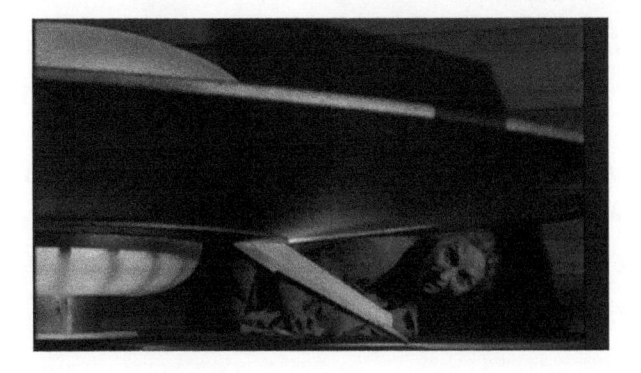

MAUGHAM, W. SOMERSET.
1874-1965.

Willie Maugham was one of the most successful of writers in the 20th century. He wrote one short story, "Rain," that made him over one million dollars in the 1920s. You could say he was the rich man's Truman Capote.

A short documentary gathers together some rare photos and film clips of his high-living. It's called Revealing Mr. Maugham. But it is mostly apologetic for his transgressions and motive to write for money.

Maugham suffered from a stammer that made him less media attractive—but like Capote, he wrote about the gossip he heard, transforming the mud in novels. He was no great writer, like many contemporaries (James Joyce, Virginia Woolf or even Noel Coward) but he made big bucks and commanded movie versions *(The Razor's Edge)*.

Being secretly gay, he never played out or up his personality like Capote. Yet, he was notorious in his world travels to seek gay pleasure spots around the world. His "secretary" was actually his lover and procurer.

Maugham learned about human nature at medical school where he studied with Dr. Bell, the model for Conan Doyle's Sherlock Holmes. And, his understanding of sexuality was scientific and ahead of its time.

He was scarred by his brother Harry's suicide over a homosexual scandal—and it may have sent Maugham into the closet for the rest of his life.

His companion Gerald Haxton helped him create Cap Ferrat, the idyllic "Fairyland," that Edna St. Vincent Millay declared one visit. Her insight is not in the film. Nor does the film tell us of the monkey gland injections to maintain his masculine vigor in old age to host boys, boys, boys.

The documentary tries hard to give Maugham literary chops, but he was interested only in fame and money, whether as a playwright or as a story writer. Yes, he wrote spy stories before LeCarre and Greene, and he was an actual spy for the British government.

Yet, he became in senility a rather unpleasant, vindictive and manipulated old fool of his new "secretary," who managed to steal everything through poisoning Maugham's old mind.

The documentary shows how one can outlive his own standards.

"The Letter."

Few people know that director William Wyler made two versions of Maugham's hothouse Ceylon plantation story of murder. The more famous one with Bette Davis was in 1941, but he followed that up with a live television version in 1956.

You don't have to wonder which is better.

With its electrifying opening two minutes, Bette Davis went into legendary status, plugging a man six times as he staggered out of her plantation estate.

The Somerset Maugham story has a juicy scandal behind the tale of who and why Leslie killed a man visiting her home while her husband was away.

Only her lawyer sees the ruthless woman behind the stitching and knitting like Madame De Farge. There seems to be a letter that could incriminate her—and it is in the possession of the dead man's wife! She wants what is a king's ransom to give back to Bette/Leslie.

Without it, her lawyer realizes she may be guilty of cold-blooded murder or at least passionate jealousy.

Filled with mood and imagery, like the full moon, jungle animal noises, and music to rile you up, this is a memorable film in many details. The TV show was a flat journalistic exercise not worthy of Maugham's tale or Wyler's reputation. It did have Anna Mae Wong as the frightful Mrs. Hammond who has the incriminating letter. Gale Sondergaard does the role in the film, and she terrified Miss Davis on and off screen. With good reason.

With a good lawyer, the letter is retrieved and evidence withheld from justice, husband, and public. Herbert Marshall always seemed to play Bette's long-suffering husband (as in *Little Foxes*).

Under pressure, the murderer seems doomed by the moonlight shining on her. You may ask yourself why she goes outside the safety of the house gates during the party to celebrate her victory over justice. Then, again, she blurts it out in one of the most famous confessions ever: "I still love the man I killed."

What a movie.

McCULLERS, CARSON.

1917-1967.

"Reflections in a Golden Eye"

Brando is horse-whipped by Miss Taylor.

When great literature meets a movie, the result is not always pleasing to author, readers, movie fans, or critics. When the cult writer Carson McCullers finally agreed that movie legend John Huston ought to tackle her novella or long short story called *Reflections in a Golden Eye,* she was thrilled.

She met with the director, wanted script approval, cast approval, and fell in love with Huston. She died before the film was released, and some think it killed her. When the story hit the screen, no one was happy.

My long-time writing collaborator, film star, actor, and Renaissance Man, Jan Merlin, jumped aboard with me to do an in-depth examination of movie making in the wild 1960s.

As a star of two television series including *Rough Riders* and *Tom Corbett: Space Cadet,* Jan also did two dozen movies and had worked with Huston, knew Brando, and had some extraordinary insights to add.

Fans of stars Elizabeth Taylor and Brando will find grotesque movie-making tales, and lovers of disasters can find our book under the title *Troubles in a Golden Eye*. The film took an incident at a small long-ago modern army fort where a man might have become a hero to his wife by killing a man stalking her, but the story reveals the grotesque truth.

After writing this movie book with Jan Merlin, I realized it was not your typical PR story or one of those fan-styled books. As writers, we know intimately the details of some of the stars and have inside information on the actual filming of this dog of a movie.

This does not always sit well with friends of the people involved, which is why this is unauthorized book angered the hangers-on and toadies of the principals. The famous dropped by during the filming process: Truman Capote, Richard Burton, and all the names of old Hollywood. If you love your gossip, there was plenty to be found in this tale.

Some people involved with this film wanted to spill the dirt, and let me tell you the dirt is here by the shovels-full. The usual jealous types can't say much except try to stop you from learning about egomaniacs like Brando, Taylor, Huston, and the cult writer McCullers.

If it makes you want to see the movie again to understand what went wrong in the production, we have done our jobs. As for me, I love the movie and enjoy sharing how it must have felt to be on the set while it was made on Long Island and Rome in 1966. Alas, the humor of the process and madness of all the participants may be lost in history's fact check. "

MILLER, ARTHUR.

1915-2005.

"The Misfits."

Arthur Miller was a great American playwright who wrote only one short story—and based it on his wife to do as a film. He adapted the story for film and one of the ultimate film directors, John Huston, came on board: he had the credentials to deal with what was considered a high-power, temperamental cast of prima donnas.

Since Arthur Miller's wife was Marilyn Monroe at the time, the film was produced despite her apparent lack of cooperation (so claimed director John Huston). She was a mess during production in terms of psychology, and the movie turned out to be her final one.

It is, nevertheless, stunning to behold.

She is luminescent and her performance seems to have been captured easily. Whether this is the real Marilyn, we presume it was the person Miller knew and the character she wanted to portray. She falls in with a bunch of people, while in Nevada for a divorce, who are outsiders, or misfits.

The all-star cast of this modern Western is legend: Monty Clift, Thelma Ritter, Eli Wallach, and Clark Gable in his last performance too. They said Marilyn's unprofessionalism taxed Gable to the point of a fatal heart attack. It seems too much hype and no evidence in the movie.

It is a strenuous movie with a bronco chasing scene out in the hot, arid desert where Gable and Monroe are both given hard conditions to play out their roles. It is a grand movie for all these reason, and every scene is geared to give the performers a golden acting moment.

Miller's script is far off his range, yet these are interesting people: sad, pathetic, lost, hopeless, and out of their element. To watch Gable dragged along the desert sand by a rampaging horse, and to see Monroe knocked down as she tries to save the wild animals from the glue factory is the stuff of grand Hollywood. Most will remember the scene in which Monroe wins a contest and bats a paddle ball 100 times on camera flawlessly.

They can't make movies like this nowadays. You don't have the talent, the Hollywood system, or the legendary figures who might come together over a literary script. This is a rare movie that cannot be judged by any normal standard.

Sad Anniversary

Was it really so long ago in August, 1962, that Marilyn died so suddenly and mysteriously? We heard the news on Sunday morning on vacation. Was it an accident or some kind of bizarre conspiracy that did her in?

She was thought to be a sad, pathetic suicide at the time of her death, body claimed by former husband Joe DiMaggio. Her last film was *the Misfits* with Clark Gable, written by her ex-husband and playwright Arthur Miller. It was extraordinary stuff. She could play light comedy or heavy tragedy *(Some Like It Hot, Bus Stop)*.

She had become emotionally erratic, fired by the studio and dismissed from movies (The outtakes of *Something's Got to Give* s how her radiant and perfect. Over an hour of film footage was reconstructed a few years back. Why did they fire her?). The career trauma seemed to explain her death—at first.

Over time, we learned she was a victim of the casting couch: with lurid stories of her promiscuity and misuse by producers and unscrupulous men (and Joan Crawford).

Then, we learned she was the victim of the President of the United States and his brother. Some even speculate that she was assassinated by the CIA because she was about to blow the whistle on political shenanigans and UFOs, state secrets she learned in her dalliances.

Now, more recently, we hear that she fought the casting couch mentality of Hollywood, walked out of movies when she was mistreated and sexually abused.

Whatever the truth, she was a luminous talent, who actually glowed on celluloid. Her career might have been on the skids because of age by the late 1960s, but we will never know whether she would have made a transformation to character actress, or into a legend as she is now.

Poor Marilyn. She was missed immediately-- and is still missed today.

A Life Taken Advantage Of...

Love, Marilyn builds its subject out of her own words, based on recently discovered diaries, jottings, poetry, and other musings written by Marilyn Monroe.

A dozen actors read her words and the words of those who knew her—those friends and associates usually caused her great consternation and pain.

Marilyn Monroe still today plays heroine and victim at once, misunderstood still, and exploited at every turn.

The footage of her acting, both on and off screen, grows more desperate. She herself regarded Marilyn as a separate creature she had to play for the media and public.

In fact, Marilyn created her own Frankenstein's Monster out of body language and platinum blonde hair that ran amok out of the Hollywood studios and was chased down by the media with cameras instead of pitchforks.

Director Liz Garbus does her best to take the luminous star and catch it falling from the firmament. Only in death has Miss Monroe touched more people than in life as a movie star.

No one who tied his wagon to Marilyn comes out of this documentary unscathed. Her two husbands, Joe DiMaggio and Arthur Miller, knew her better than anyone else in the world—

and knew her not at all. In later years they regretted the way they treated her.

No one attempts to explain why Monroe wrote down so many feelings in couplets and free verse on dozens of pieces of paper. Was she planning to write a script? Did she plan an autobiography later in life? Was it merely an attempt to exorcize her demons by putting them on paper?

No one in 20th century America comes close to her iconography and her ability to become a goddess walking in our midst for a few years. (We see James Dean as a male counterpart.) She glowed on screen with some magic that defies explanation.

This little documentary, using her own words, may be the closest attempt to doing her justice and giving her the platform she may have hoped to employ if her life had not been snuffed out so young.

Marilyn herself pegged the trouble to trusting too easily, too many, too often. How sad indeed.

Patsy Monroe?

In a new documentary called *Marilyn Monroe Declassified,* director and writer Paul Davids in 2016 tackled the thorny subject of the probable suicide (its official designation) almost 60 years later.

He takes much archival footage and tries to find rare insights to give a background in his premise that it was more likely her death was an improbable suicide."

No doubt that even decades later, Marilyn is a glowing and beautiful icon, transcending time and place. She may be up there in a few thousand years with women like Helen of Troy. Yes, legends easily pass into mythology with a background like Marilyn.

This film purports to examine both FBI and CIA documents only recently released to public scrutiny.

Using some fairly reputable scholars and researchers, the film veers off the standard biography patter for the final 20 minutes or so when the revelations about affairs with the Kennedy brothers (President and Attorney General) devolves into a mob contracted hit to embarrass the Kennedy Administration, led by the CIA guru and demonologist, James Angleton.

Sam Giancana, who believed the Kennedys betrayed him, was an eager contractor for Angleton. All stones could be unturned and thrown into the ocean when used. You may well ask yourself why it took 4 hours to call the police to report Marilyn was dead by her housekeeper (allegedly a CIA agent). After that, all bets are off.

The connection to Kennedy revealing to Monroe about the truth of the Roswell incident is documented in CIA/FBI reports. Whether true or not, she believed it and was prepared to use it, but the CIA was not about to accept that reality.

This documentary may seem to have gone off the rails, but it also seems grounded in the horrors that not even *Ancient Aliens* will tackle. It appears Oswald was not the only Patsy in a conspiracy-ruled world.

P

POE, EDGAR ALLEN.
1809-1849.

"Buried Alive."

Actor Denis O'Hare

When PBS tackles the life of Edgar Allan Poe in a re-enacted biographical documentary, you may have something special—or not.

In this case, the superior production values and participation of actor Denis O'Hare as Poe is high-end, though the actor is a bit long-in-the-tooth for the role. The film is *Edgar Allan Poe: Buried Alive.*

What's buried alive, akin to one of his plots, is his sordid lifestyle and the likely truth.

The problem with Poe, and with the hypothesis of the film, is that he was the victim of bad press: not mad, not a drug addict, *etc*. Alas, that is not-quite honest. You could accurately say he lived up to his press clippings or musty grave stories.

Poe was an American master in terms of knowing that he had to become his own character, much like Hemingway and other writers, to play himself as flesh and blood page turner to be a social media darling.

Poe's mother was an actress—and he certainly inherited her stage presence. He loved to present his poetry in narrative drama on stage. His "Raven" was to die for, one hot ticket. O'Hare recites a few lines, making us wish the entire show was comprised of his reading Poe poetry.

Eddie, as his experts call him with all too much familiarity, was combative, especially when drunk—and he did drink, like many talented authors. The so-called experts cited in interviews are mostly novelists who admire his style, and act as apologists for his bad behavior.

And bad it is by modern standards. There is no way to sugar-coat his marriage to a 13-year old cousin (faked ID marriage license said 21), and the experts here in the #MeToo age are winking and nodding, even the women fans of Poe.

Having middle-age O'Hare (age 55) play Poe at 27 with his interest in the pre-pubescent girl makes it even more lascivious. You can't sweep the stench of pedophilia under the grave or under the floorboards.

Poe's mad, unreliable narrators and tales of murderers may nevermore be disparaged, but Poe himself is the epitome of one of his horrors. His mysterious death at age 40 stands as his greatest unfinished tale.

This is nevertheless a brilliant tell-tale heart-felt documentary. Well, let's at least quoth the Raven.

"Tell-Tale Heart."

Poe's Big Three: Karloff, Price, and Lorre in The Raven.

We have lost track over how many bad versions of the story are out there, mostly low-budget, 20-minute versions. Actors often produce the picture and want to star, no matter their age or acting ability.

If the performers don't measure up in a Poe tale, you are dead in the water, as it were.

Most of the proto-typical psychos of this story are in over their heads and lack the vocal range or sophistication with dialogue of the 19th century. You really need a classically trained Shakespearean actor to either read Poe or play his dialogue.

That seems to be out of the question—unless you start to look at the spate of bad movies based on a variety of Poe stories. Vincent Price and Boris Karloff are frequently stars of over-extended poverty row studio pictures from American International.

You have a good actor and a bad script, poor direction, and melodrama instead of psychological terror.

Poor Poe. He can't win the movie sweepstakes, and we are still awaiting any version of anything. We did see one excellent rendition of "The Raven," which is a prose poem, not a short story.

So, like Mark Twain whose novels are usually made into movies, not his short pieces, Edgar Allen Poe has an award named after him for other writers to win, but Poe is the loser in the moviedom productions.

POLLACK, LOUIS.
1904-1964.

"Breakdown."
And Leave the Driving to Hitch....

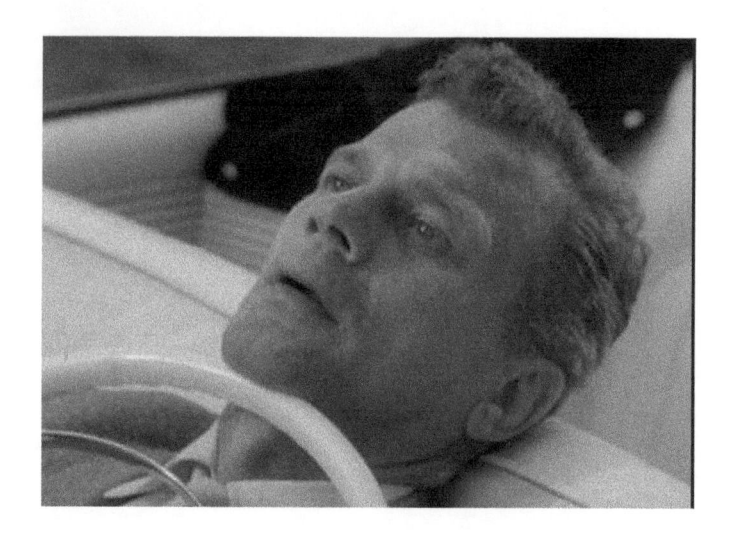

"Breakdown" brought Joseph Cotten back together with his old friend Alfred Hitchcock for a half-hour television episode that would send chills down the spine of anyone thinking of driving down to Florida alone.

Once again, Hitchcock played with his words. His breakdown could be a fancy sports car in disrepair, or a man in mental exhaustion. In the case of the show, it could be a word for all seasons.

A ruthless business tycoon (Cotten) fires people over the telephone without remorse and is shocked when one accountant begins to cry piteously. Contempt is his best reaction, finding such weakness to be beneath his attention.

Yet, when a bulldozer working with a chain gang hits his car, he is left paralyzed behind the wheel, looking to the world like a dead man. The steering wheel has crushed his chest, or so concludes every witness.

Not one takes his pulse, so convinced are they of his demise. Thus begins his voice-over thoughts as he is robbed, stripped, has his identity taken, but is able to tap his finger to alert the world of his living carcass.

It is to no avail as the shroud is put over him, and he is left in a morgue. Hitchcock pulled out all the stops of fear on this one— from dying, from being buried alive, to fear of loneliness in its ultimate form.

Augurs and omens dominate the first few moments, perhaps giving a clue or two about the fate and character of Cotton's heartless protagonist.

Cotten must act without benefit of any movement, tic, or facial acknowledgement. He is up to the task, a monumental endeavor for an actor to act dead.

PROULX, ANNIE.

1935-

I am Heath Ledger

Derik Murray has put together a series of "I am.." documentaries. They are intimate, unflinching, and hypnotic films about subjects with charisma and cult interest. Something went wrong along the way on this one called *I am Heath Ledger*.

So it is not surprising to find Heath Ledger being given the mythic figure treatment. He is no James Dean because he was filled with *joie d'vivre* and was a man with a cause and a mission.

Ledger said openly that he was on a mission to push his artistic feelings to the limit. He surrounded himself with his Australian friends from boyhood as an entourage for the most part, but there were no naysayers in the bunch. There was also no one to help him discipline himself. He was brilliant, a chess prodigy and potential major film director.

Going without sleep and pushing his physical limits, Heath Ledger was a whirling dervish of inspired talents. He was into music and film in particular, but showed unlimited artistic abilities. He took endless videos of himself, almost each snippet a movie in miniature. He was observing and teaching himself what reactions worked in a role.

He managed to improve with each role, but seemingly his happy demeanor hinted at a less satisfying deeper sense. His marriage fell apart, and he increasingly covered his beautiful body with tattoos. He used himself as a laboratory for life.

He spoke that he had limited time, like so many music and movie legends who went beyond before age 30. Was he prescient, or just a workaholic?

Heath left several stunning performances in *Brokeback Mountain* and *The Dark Knight*, but his colleagues do not line up to appear in this film tribute—only family and close friends are anguished and full of love. Naomi Watts and Ang Lee speak about him, but the film turns on the achievements of his friends, rather than on Heath finally.

The spin of final repeated clips at the end of the documentary without words may be more telling as the film seems to spin away too.

"Brokeback Mountain."

A story about two cowpokes in the 1960s was bound to come across as uncomfortable for many lovers of Westerns. It was always acceptable for unspoken homoerotic bonds between men out West to be underplayed. Many viewers were never ready for the openly sexual relationship of two men: as played by Heath Ledger and Jake Gyllenhaal.

If you ever want an argument that people want their privacy not invaded, this movie works for both characters and audience. The Lone Ranger and Tonto may have been consenting adults, but as long as no one talked about it, then it was okay.

Brokeback Mountain, directed by Ang Lee, is likely unpopular for its subject, and it lost a Best Picture Oscar to a lesser film because of audience discomfort over the classic male figures out of their usual stereotypes.

Brokeback Mountain is not exactly Shangri-La, but it serves as a refuge for gay men in a hostile world. You want to laugh at Proulx's tale for calling the closet-case Ennis (dropping the P). But that's the trouble: one is more open and careless, and the other is the ultimate loner.

The actors are about as on the money as you could find: masculine and attractive and the spell under which they fall, a once in a lifetime love affair, may be romantic and unrealistic. Yet, for that world in those pre-liberated days, men married and carried on in sheer falsity. So, it was for these two whose annual fishing trips were their true happiness.

Alas, they could not quit each other. And that led to their sad story. It's hard to know what powerful force most devastates them: social pressure, economics, or simply their biological urges. That question is a close second to whether this is a

Western or a gay genre movie. It is neither fish, nor fowl, and its fans and detractors have equal shooting time.

It is a tragic, sensitive film already falling between the cracks of movie history. The book is half the length of a novel and a bit longer than a short story. It just doesn't fit in that category either.

S

SHELLEY, MARY,

nee Wollstonecraft

1797-1851

"Frankenstein."

Stars Relax!

The Monster became an archetype when director James Whale created his bizarre version of the Shelley story. Imagining the creature would have an influence on Hollywood history. Only Lon Chaney as the Hunchback of Notre Dame and Bette Davis as Baby Jane Hudson would make such an indelible impression.

Frankenstein defies the ancient year it was made in 1931.

The performance of Boris Karloff under the tons of makeup might make him lost forever (like Claude Rains being invisible for an entire movie), but. The opposite occurred. His billing as "?" demanded that he become a face to be seen.

His performance under the disadvantage of immovable makeup was sensitive and powerfully emotional. That alone demanded recognition.

SHORT STORIES INTO FILM

Director James Whale gave the Shelley story a completely off-the-wall melodrama of actors out of control: Colin Clive as the mad scientist and Dwight Frye as the trollish Fritz, though everyone thinks he is Igor (that was another movie parody).

With a series of episodic encounters (a blind man, a child, and finally with Clive at the windmill), you have actors with faces to behold.

Every moment of the film is frightfully apt, from cutting down hanged men, to the brilliant electric storm that causes Colin Clive to cry out, "It's alive," you have something Mary Shelly might have stepped back and watched with horror. Her story came to life in ways that literature often rejects.

Unsung Creative Force!

Wolf Man Credit!

What a delicious untold story! A Greek immigrant boy comes to Hollywood and his creative juices give us the most famous monster makeup creatures of 20th century movies. Check out *Jack Pierce: Maker of Monsters*.

Like all the people who came to Hollywood in its infancy, they were self-made and their artistic sense was equally applied to their own lives. Jack Pierce did it all—from stunts, to camera operator, to director, but found his niche in applying makeup to the stars.

When Lon Chaney bailed on playing *Dracula*,

Jack was thwarted by Bela Lugosi who had his own ideas. However, it was on *Frankenstein* that he grew into legend, spending months researching how the creature should look. It led to a plethora of famous monsters: *The Mummy, the Invisible Man, the Bride of Frankenstein,* but he was head of Universal and worked on making beautiful women more stunning.

The Mummy makeup took 8 hours to apply and another hour to remove. If Karloff was uncomplaining, no wonder a friendship between them developed.

Pierce's makeup effects often terrified the naïve audiences of the 1930s. He was Universal Studio's master: responsible for all the horrors up to 1947. When they were about to gather all the monsters for a comedy, Abbot and Costello meet, Jack was fired, but his makeup style was maintained.

Later, a myth grew around *Frankenstein* that James Whale, director, created the face: not true. Karloff always gave credit to his friend, Pierce. You can thank the movie and book *Gods and Monsters* for the misinformation.

Always an actor at heart, Jack wore a lab coat in the makeup room, which certainly intimidated Elsa Lanchester, who was the Bride of the monster. She recalled it thirty years later in less than happy terms. Jack did Lon Chaney, Jr., as *Wolf Man*, Dracula, and Frankenstein, over the years. That too was not a good relationship.

If they needed a star to age from 30 to 80, Jack Pierce could make it happen for a generation. One of his last makeup jobs was for *Mr. Ed*, the talking horse, hired by his friend from Universal, Arthur Lubin.

When Jack died in 1969, almost no one from the movie world came to his funeral. Fascinating bio of a nearly forgotten figure of film history.

Fraser, Olyphant, or Caviezel?

As part of our continuing shock at how many years have passed since certain minor classic films have been around, we were stunned to note that it is nearly that long since Ian McKellan played the director of *Frankenstein,* In 1957, before his suicide.

James Whale was gay, and the Bill Condon film is based on novelized account of his last days in 1957 and is titled *Gods and Monsters*. Partly owing to John Hurt playing a literary critic stalking a teen heart-throb in *Love and Death on Long Island* the year before, we had McKellan with a sunset crush on his gardener.

How true is it all? At least we were not treated to one of those disclaimers, "Based on a true story."

Whale had long since left the Hollywood sound stage, partly owing to box office poison. He had made some literate and funny horror films that stand the test of time: *Frankenstein* and *Bride* thereof.

With his mind slipping away from a stroke or some form of Alzheimer's Disease, he puts his attention on Brendan Fraser, a most handsome young yardman with a flat top hairdo that is just too preciously reminiscent of the Monster designed by Whale in 1931.

Fraser, at the time, was part of a trio of actors who could have been interchangeable in the role: Timothy Olyphant and Jim Caviezel were the other two. All the same age and style.

McKellan is, as always, brilliant and plays off Lynn Redgrave as his unattractive housekeeper. He puts the moves on the unwilling Fraser, but it is all subterfuge to force the homophobic former Marine into killing him and putting him out of his misery.

A coda to the sensitive, episodic incidents in Whale's final days, is perhaps the weakest link in the movie as Condon had no idea how to end it, that is otherwise a powerful biographical movie.

Horrors' Start

Byronic Vampire?

As one expert notes, these personages in the title are the twin pillars of modern horror—more than a century of monstrous concepts: life coming out of the dead.

A Dark and Stormy Night is the subtitle of this intriguing documentary that uses the words of five people thrown together at Villa Diodati in 1816. This illustrious group of young bohemians of the era included two immortal poets, Shelly and Byron, their paramours, and their young doctor.

For those without a proper literary historical perspective, Lord Byron challenged his housemates one stormy night to write a ghost story. They had the summer without light, as it was called, to do it. In the United States, it was called "the year without summer."

Switzerland and the world suffered in 1816 from a year without proper summer: crops failed, storms cascaded around the Earth because of a super-volcanic explosion in the Pacific. So with a constant barrage of thunderstorms and lighting candles in mid-afternoon, the crew of Mary Shelley, Percy Shelly, Dr. J.M. Polidori (Byron's travel companion) and Claire (Byron's latest stalker/groupie) took up the task.

They allegedly urged, critiqued, and drove each other on to come up with a horrifying tale. Mrs. Shelley wrote about the modern Prometheus, Frankenstein, and Dr. Polidori came up with the first elegant, aristocratic vampire that set the mold for Dracula in fifty years.

Some wags believed that Byron wrote the original outline, and Polidori, pretender to the poet, stole it and finished it.

The scandalous summer featured rumors of drugs, sex, and bizarre carrying on, which suited the weirdness of the weather in 1816.

Of course, burning the candle as it were all day and all night, led to an early demise of Polidori in 1821, Shelley in 1822, and Byron in 1824. Mary Shelley lived to see her story take on a life in literature—and years later realized she had survived the ghosts of Diodati.

Fascinating documentary with earnest re-enactors, trying to avoid their sexual peccadilloes. It seems almost preposterous that those so young could produce such masterpieces of literature.

It's a story worth watching.

A Dark & Stormy Movie

Polidori, Shelley, and Byron, aka Spall, Sands, and Byrne

If you want to learn about the dark and stormy night in 1816 that resulted in the creation of *Frankenstein* and *Dracula* by Lord Byron's pals, you might look elsewhere.

Ken Russell's hothouse and nuthouse movie about Percy and Mary Shelley and Lord Byron is pure *Gothic* nonsense. As was the style of Russell back in 1987, you had a psychedelic version of biography and history. It is not satisfactory.

The cast is somewhat exemplary: Gabriel Byrne as lame Byron, Julian Sands as pretty Shelley, Timothy Spall as off-putting Dr.

Polidori, and Natasha Richardson as demure Mary! Wow, you almost expect the acting alone will carry the film.

However, the director hijacks every moment and even has cast members chewing on rats. We thought the film turned into that rat-festival movie *Willard*. And, inexplicable pythons wrap around suits of armor. Yep, it's Ken Russell.

Instead of a dark and stormy night where these highly creative people choose to write great books, we have a literal ghost story. The demons are really around every corner. You almost feel sorry for the servants who basically take a powder during the latter part of the movie to avoid these koo-koo birds.

The summer without sun inspired the writing of Frankenstein and Dracula. Byron took credit for Polidori's work, and Byron couldn't write prose. The stepsister of Mary is around for crazy moments in which the sexual peccadilloes of the characters is tested.

We have more than your usual homoerotic connections between the men, including some fairly passionate kisses, but Julian Sands was never prettier. Gabriel Byrne seems to have bigger breasts than the women stars. Timothy Spall is actually slim.

The film becomes increasingly erratic and difficult to watch, as befits what did in the style of Ken Russell ultimately. We had hoped to see something truly fascinating, but not quite on the level of a train wreck.

Another Dark & Stormy Movie

Gang sits around on a dark & stormy night!

Someone read the Henry James novella *Aspern Papers* and found inspiration to make a movie about the real people (Mary, Lord Byron, and Percy Shelley) that were fictionalized for literary movies, but made flesh for a biopic.

Elle Fanning and Douglas Booth make for a beautiful couple of poet Shelley and his young companion Mary Godwin. They are a couple of free-love, free spirits. Throw in the stepsister of Mary (Claire Claremont) who is moved to seduce Lord Byron (Tom Sturridge) who greets Shelley with a kiss on the lips. Here we have the roots of *The Aspern Papers*.

It's all the more intriguing because about ten years ago a lost manuscript of Claire was discovered in which she unloaded on the Romantic poets for their cruel attitudes.

This movie features Mary Shelley keeping her husband's love letters and poems, savoring them. Of course, it was Claire who lived until 1879 and might have inspired Henry James to write his nasty novella about the mystery behind the free-love advocates.

The Shelleys meet Byron around the same time that Mary becomes fascinated with galvanism or electrifying dead bodies to bring them back to life.

The biopic is flavorful and masterly filmed, even giving us the dark and stormy night that Byron challenged them to write a ghost story. Dr. Polidori writes the first true vampire novel, and Mary writes *Frankenstein: or the Modern Prometheus*.

No one believes either was capable of such a feat—and their works were at first attributed to Shelley and Byron, respectively.

Byron comes across as a sniveling snake in this film, and Shelley is the whoremaster Mary's father accuses him of being.

If you want to see the real *Aspern Papers* that Henry James alluded to in his covert way, this could be it.

SHEPHERD, JEAN.
1921-1999.

"A Christmas Story."

Blessed with a radio announcer's voice and the talent of a raconteur and wit, Jean Shepherd could spin anecdotes better than anyone since Mark Twain.

His collection of five short stories was developed into a Christmas holiday tradition, though the original film release was a bomb! *In God We Trust, All Others Pay Cash*, became the story of Ralphie wanting a rifle for Christmas. It is beyond nostalgia. It has become ingrained Americana.

Twain's short stories fell short when it came to movies, but Shepherd is the master of a pre-TV America.

Set in the late 1940s when life was about to become the high-water mark of the world, life is world of radio contests, having a dopey brother, and hot-tempered father.

Each step he takes, Ralphie seems to lose innocence: whether it is the fakery of a decoder ring, school performances, radio serials, and Santa Claus. He is disappointed by each. He sees his father win "a major award," that is a hideous and cheap lamp that his mother "accidentally" breaks when they are out of glue.

His mother is against him having an air rifle that will likely shoot out his eye. Yet, this is a story so filled with charm and delight that it is just another step along the path of a safe, middle-class life, as intoned safely by the narrator.

To everyone's surprise, this was a cross multi-generational movie and story that met with wide-spread love and good feelings. Your spiritual journey in life should always be like Ralphie's.

SIMENON, GEORGES.

1903-1989.

"Man on the Eiffel Tower."

Laughton in detective hero mode.

SHORT STORIES INTO FILM

Making a motion picture on location in Europe in the late 1940s was done masterfully by Carol Reed and *The Third Man*. Trying to emulate that came a Paris-based production called *Man on the Eiffel Tower*.

Filmed entirely in Paris and in color, it was meant to be a travelogue to whet the appetite of arm-chair tourists and fans of Hercule Poirot, with a bad stand-in, Inspector Maigret.

It should have been interesting and one of the post-war gems. Alas, despite car rides through the streets of Paris, lunch on the Eiffel Tower, and a climax in which the supervillain plans to jump off with breathtaking views, the movie is a mess.

It is a Maigret mystery with Laughton as a slightly irascible, overweight, curmudgeon. He is perfect and does his usual schtick in routine fashion, playing opposite a foppish and dissipated looking Franchot Tone. Laughton is not Hercule (who is Belgian, we know), but might have had trouble with the fastidious role.

Taking over directing duties when Laughton threatened to quit the movie (and you can see why he may have considered it), is Burgess Meredith. We see him here a decade before he played a similar role on *Twilight Zone* in a classic episode about a man wearing thick eyeglasses.

Also aboard is empty-suit leading man Robert Hutton, also looking less boyish than usual.

Perhaps the source material of the famous detective failed them, but the movie leaps and bounds to try to capture the flavor of Paris from rooftop chases to taxi rides around the ambiance of the Left Bank. It is mostly American actors or Brits pretending to be as French as the actual settings.

It just didn't work, and throw in a music score that is intrusive and overbearing, and you have undercut drama, suspense, performances, and plot.

What a disappointment. This film is a classic of bad movie-making. The producer tried to bury it by hiding all the prints, but failed.

SMITH, F.J.

"One More Mile To Go."

Before Mrs. Jacoby Sleeps with the Fishes

Two years before *Psycho*, Hitchcock did a dry run on his television show. He had toyed with the idea of an oddball, living with an older woman (wife, mother, sister, aunt) and used it in Shadow of a Doubt with the quirky neighbor Herbie Hawkins (Hume Cronyn) whose sick mother seemed a smothering influence. He is a version of Norman Bates.

Sam Jacoby (David Wayne) fights in the picture window of his rural home. It looks like a small screen TV with the sound turned down low. Mrs. Jacoby (Louise Larrabee) is never identified beyond that. Sam does not wear a wedding ring.

For eight minutes (an eternity on television), dialogue is muted and unheard, like a silent movie—or worse like listening to an argument in the next apartment by putting a glass up against the wall to hear indistinct sounds. The characters argue loudly until Sam picks up a fireplace iron and clobbers the little lady.

Immediately we end up inside the home and with the sound on full. Sam seems to make an instant decision to rid himself of the incriminating dead body.

In the attached garage he stuffs her into a burlap sack, not a shower curtain, and finds enough heavy iron tools to sink the body in a local lake. He must only drive there in the dark to dump the deceased.

We have a similar car ride as both Norman has a dead Marion Crane in the trunk of her newly purchased car. Sam will not sink both the car and body in a lake, but merely deposit his cargo.

Along the way a moon-faced motorcycle cop stops him and sticks his face into the driver's window, much like the *Psycho* cop. He merely seems menacing, as he helpfully announces the taillight is out. He is willing to open the trunk and fix it for Sam.

Their cat and mouse continues to a local gas station, with the nervous Wayne doing anything to prevent the trunk from opening. Escaping once, he is relieved and on his way to the lake again when the persistent motorcycle cop shows up again.

SHORT STORIES INTO FILM

If anticipation, anxiety, uncertainty, and the curse of fate ever merged into a better twenty-two minutes directed by Hitchcock, we have not seen it.

STEPHENSON, CARL.
1893- c. 1954.

"Leinengen Vs The Ants."

Antsy Attackers!

The Naturalistic horror tale was given a far more salacious name for the movies: *The Naked Jungle*.

Like Hitchcock's *The Birds*, you have a mass of nature turning against humankind with destructive force that suggests an apocalypse. And, like these kind of horror movies, the suspense builds until the final half-hour when the creatures go on a rampage.

Here you have Charlton Heston as the star and main antagonist to the army of devouring ants. How can they win against Moses,

SHORT STORIES INTO FILM

Ben Hur, Jean LaFitte, and Gordon of Khartoum? Well, it's touch and go for a while.

The horror elements include close-ups of ants pouring across the screen and creating rafts to cross a river to attack people. They can eat the flesh off your body in five minutes, according to experts advising Heston. Yikes.

The disturbing sound of their crunch as they munch was created by George Pal, special effects expert.
We have to laud these insects for having the temerity to take on the forces of human social systems, economic exploitation of South American natives, and the biologic order of being at the bottom of the pecking order.

In this world, before the 21st century recognition of the Earth's fragility, you have the ultimate punishment for crimes against Nature.

Smart characters like the Commissioner (actor William Conrad) evacuate before the main action. Heston plans to defend his turf, whatever the cost.

If you believe in the survival of the fittest, you probably wonder why there was no sequel to this tale of beasts on a mission. You likely think beating back the ant hill will change people, but we doubt it has. The lesson of Stephenson's 1938 story may be quite different 100 years later.

W

WOOLRICH, CORNELL
1903-1968.

"Four O'Clock."

SHORT STORIES INTO FILM

Hitchcock lent his talents out to another television show in 1958. He filmed the effort in the summer of 1957 in his favorite studio and closed set. He directed an episode of the series *Suspicion*, which he also served as executive producer. Unlike his own show in its early days, this allowed him to direct a full-hour episode, actually about fifty minutes in length.

Finding a story from Cornell Woolrich who gave him *Rear Window*, Hitchcock gathered together Nancy Kelly and E.G. Marshall, two well-respected actors who had not quite made the major leagues yet.

They were the Steppes—Paul and Fran, not exactly happily married as Paul was of the mind that his wife was cuckolding him with a young man. Before you can say divorce lawyer, Paul steps out of line after eavesdropping on his wife with young handsome Dave (Richard Long), another in a long line of dashing black-haired ne'er-do wells. What Paul fails to realize is that this is his wife's black sheep brother whose identity she has kept secret from everyone.

Paul decides to give his wife a final split. He creates a time bomb that will go off exactly at 4 o'clock in the afternoon while he is at the office where he repairs clocks. It seems time and tide wait not for him.

Of course, Hitchcock had learned an important lesson from the movie he had directed in England over twenty years earlier. And, he intended to right a wrong, or blow up another story in the making.

If the Master had a vision with this film, it was the irony of the countdown to the explosion, not quite going the way Mr. Steppe had planned. You see, thugs rob him and tie him up in the cellar with his bomb. He can only wait and hope his wife will come downstairs and rescue them both.

The ticking bomb is enough to cause anyone to sweat bullets.

Dr. William Russo taught Short Story into Film among his many popular film courses for several decades at Curry College. This book is an extension of that course. Not every great writer wrote short stories (or long shorts), or had them produced into motion pictures. This listing of films and authors is arbitrary and selective.

CPSIA information can be obtained
at www.ICGtesting.com
Printed in the USA
LVHW030811211221
706747LV00005B/336